INV 304950 A
5 MAY /09

DIRTY
LITTLE
SECRETS

D1166609

LVG 405950
5 MAY '09

ESSA PUBLIC LIBRARY

Entrepreneur
POCKET GUIDES

DIRTY LITTLE SECRETS

What the
CREDIT
BUREAUS
Won't Tell You

Entrepreneur Press and
Jason R. Rich

EP
Entrepreneur.
Press

Editorial Director: Jere L. Calmes
Advisory Editor: Jack Savage
Cover Design: Beth Hansen-Winter
Production and Composition: Eliot House Productions

© 2006 by Entrepreneur Media Inc.
All rights reserved.
Reproduction or translation of any part of this work beyond that permitted by Section 107 or 108 of the 1976 United States Copyright Act without permission of the copyright owner is unlawful. Requests for permission or further information should be addressed to the Business Products Division, Entrepreneur Media Inc.

This publication is designed to provide accurate and authoritative information in regard to the subject matter covered. It is sold with the understanding that the publisher is not engaged in rendering legal, accounting or other professional services. If legal advice or other expert assistance is required, the services of a competent professional person should be sought.

Library of Congress Cataloging-in-Publication Data
    Rich, Jason.
        Dirty little secrets: what the credit bureaus won't tell you/by Entrepreneur Press and Jason R. Rich.
        p.   cm.

    ISBN13: 978-1-59918-014-4
    ISBN10: 1-59918-014-6 (alk. paper)
        1. Credit bureaus—United States. 2. Consumer credit—United States. I. Entrepreneur Press. II. Title.
    HG3751.7.R53 2006
    332.7—dc22   2006011757

Printed in Canada
12 11 10 09 08   10 9 8 7 6 5 4

Contents

Chapter 3
Obtaining Your Credit Report and Credit Score 47

Chapter 4
How to Update or Fix Your Credit Report 75

Chapter 5

Ten Strategies to Improve Your Credit
Report and Boost Your Credit Score 99

Acknowledgments

I am very proud to be working with Entrepreneur Press on its new *Personal Finance Pocket Guides* series. I hope you, the reader, find this book helpful on your quest to establish, rebuild, and manage your credit.

Thanks to Jere Calmes, Karen Thomas, and Ronald Young at Entrepreneur for inviting me to work on this project.

On a personal note, my never-ending love and gratitude goes out to my close friends—Ferras, Mark, and Ellen (as well as Ellen's family), who are all extremely important people in my life. I'd also like to thank my family for all of their support and give a shout out to my Yorkshire Terrier "Rusty" (www.MyPalRusty.com). Yes, he has his own web site, so please check it out!

Preface

Nobody wants to be known among their creditors and lenders as a deadbeat. No one intentionally sets out to accumulate so much debt that it becomes virtually impossible for them to eventually pay it off and get back on their feet financially. Yet, every year, millions of people find themselves experiencing dire financial problems.

Sure, there are many reasons financial problems can occur. Many of these reasons are often beyond our control, such as a sudden illness, a medical emergency, or getting laid off from a job, which leads to a sudden loss or dramatic reduction in income, the inability to pay one's bills, and cover living expenses. Plenty of people, however, simply mismanage their finances, can't control their spending, and choose to live outside of their financial means by overutilizing credit cards until they're maxed out.

Whatever the reason is for your financial woes, it's important to take the following steps to begin remedying your situation:

1. Carefully analyze your situation so you know exactly where you stand right now.
2. Develop a comprehensive plan to begin fixing the problem.
3. Begin paying your bills on time and paying off past due accounts.
4. In the months and years ahead, stick to your plan to insure a positive outcome.
5. Learn how to prevent a similar situation from happening again and take the necessary financial planning and budgeting steps to ensure you'll remain financially stable in the future.

As if experiencing financial problems isn't enough, it's important to understand how these problems can and ultimately will lead to credit problems that will impact you over the long term. When you begin paying your bills late, skipping payments, and overutilizing your credit cards, for example, this information gets reported to the credit reporting agencies (more commonly known as credit bureaus). The information in turn, gets added to your credit report in the form of trade lines containing negative information.

The information on your credit report is then used by the credit reporting agencies to calculate your credit score (which is also known as your FICO Score or your VantageScore). You'll learn the difference between these scores in Chapter 2. Your credit score is then utilized by your current and potential lenders and creditors to determine your credit worthiness.

People with excellent credit ultimately get offered the best credit cards, loans, and financing offers with the lowest fees and interest rates. Those who have developed average or below average credit wind up paying much higher fees and interest rates in order to obtain the same credit cards and lending privileges as someone with excellent credit (someone with a history of paying all of their bills on time and successfully managing their credit card debt).

People who ultimate destroy their credit ratings and earn below average credit scores will eventually be denied credit and loans, which means obtaining credit cards, mortgages, student loans, car loans, home equity loans, home improvement loans, store financing, or other types of credit at either impossible or extremely costly rates.

Because we're living in a society that relies so heavily on the use of credit, it's vital that you learn how to properly manage the credit you have, protect your credit rating, build a positive credit history, and discover how to best utilize your available credit in the future. If you've already made mistakes that have lead to a poor credit score and negative information appearing on your credit reports, it's important to begin taking steps to fix the situation. The negative information currently listed on your credit reports could remain there for seven to 15 years and impact your future financial stability for many years to come.

Dirty Little Secrets is an easy-to-read and understand guide that will help you better understand how credit works; manage your credit; work toward getting negative but accurate information removed from your credit reports; understand what your credit score is and how it's calculated; and teach you strategies for boosting your credit score. From this book, you'll also learn how to analyze and then improve your personal credit situation; the steps to take when preparing to apply for a mortgage, car loan, or some type of major purchase; and you'll learn where to turn for help if your credit situation has gotten so far out of control that you don't have the knowledge or resources to turn the situation around yourself.

Finally, this book offers a handful of in-depth interviews with credit experts from several of the credit reporting agencies (credit bureaus), as well as from Fair Isaac Corporation (the company responsible for creating and implementing the credit scoring system). From these people, you'll discover insider tips for managing your credit, improving the information listed on your credit report, and how to boost your credit score.

Don't be fooled! Managing, and if necessary, rebuilding your credit can be a complex and sometimes confusing process. It's also something that can seldom be done quickly.

This book will teach you exactly what to do to improve your credit situation and properly manage your credit, but if your credit score has already dropped to below 500, for example, it will realistically be many months or potentially several years before you can expect your credit score to rise above 650. (A score of 650 or higher puts you in the "average credit" or "good credit" category, whereas a credit score over 750 puts you in the "excellent credit" category.)

You've probably seen all kinds of ads for companies that can quickly "repair" your credit or have negative but accurate information permanently removed from your credit report. In reality, these services are often scams or companies perpetuating some type of fraud. From this book, you will learn the process for having your credit report modified, and discover what information can be changed and how to go about getting your credit reports corrected or updated by properly negotiating with your creditors and lenders and initiating disputes with the credit reporting agencies when it's appropriate.

From this book, you'll also learn the terminology you need to properly manage your credit and learn about a wide range of free and inexpensive resources available to you online that will help you discover even more about properly managing and rebuilding your credit. The "Tips" and "Warnings" scattered throughout this book will help bring important, money- and time-saving information to your attention and help you avoid common mistakes consumers make when dealing with their credit.

What you won't learn from this book is how to manage your personal finances, balance your checkbook, manage your investments, or develop and implement a personal or family budget. This book focuses exclusively on building, rebuilding, and maintaining good credit. You'll find other books in the *Entrepreneur Personal Finance Pocket Guide* series that focus on a wide range of topics that can help you earn more money, better manage your finances and improve your financial stability.

Dirty Little Secrets was written to provide you with an introduction to the importance of credit, and how credit fits into your financial life. This book will provide the core information you need, but it's only a start. As you'll discover, building, rebuilding, and maintaining good credit will require an ongoing effort and careful planning on your part. Although there are many quick and easy strategies you can use to "fix" some credit-related problems, in order to ensure good or excellent credit, you'll need to adopt a comprehensive approach to your spending, money management, and credit management techniques.

It's important to understand that changes are always happening in the credit industry, and that the credit reporting agencies (credit bureaus), creditors, lenders, banks, and other financial institutions are always adapting. Even the complex mathematical formula used to calculate your credit score is constantly being modified to reflect the latest consumer trends and the needs of creditors and lenders. In recent years, for example, new laws have been implemented allowing consumers free annual access to a copies of their credit reports from each of the three major credit reporting agencies.

In early 2006 (while this book was being written), an entirely new credit scoring system, called the VantageScore, was introduced and began being implemented. This scoring system could, at some point in the future, change the way your credit score is calculated and thus alter the decision-making process of lenders and creditors. It's too soon to determine if this new credit-scoring system will be widely implemented, or if the FICO scoring system, which has been around for decades, will remain the most widely used system among creditors, lenders, and other institutions. This book explains what you need to know, and offers details about free resources where you can obtain the very latest information to learn how it impacts you.

There's no better time than the present to begin securing your financial future by building, rebuilding, and properly managing your credit. This book will show you exactly how this can be done, even if you don't consider yourself to be financially savvy and even have trouble balancing your checkbook.

—Jason R. Rich
www.JasonRich.com

CHAPTER 1

Credit Reports 101
What You Must Know

WHAT'S IN THIS CHAPTER

> An introduction to what a credit report is and what information is on it.

> Details about where the information listed on your credit report comes from, who puts it there, and how long it stays.

> How your credit report impacts your financial life.

Understanding Credit

It's impossible to watch TV, listen to the radio, or read newspapers and magazines and not see and hear advertisements promoting incredible financing deals for mortgages, car loans, consumer electronics, or major appliances. The ads make statements like:

- "This weekend only, receive one year of interest-free financing on all new major appliance purchases."
- "Lease a new car today for less than $400 per month, with no money down."
- "Receive an introductory rate of 0 percent financing for six months when you apply for a new credit card today."

These deals all sound enticing. However, there's always fine print that states that these amazing offers are only available to qualified consumers with excellent credit. Someone with a less than stellar credit history, but who is still credit worthy, can expect to pay higher interest rates and extra fees. For people with poor credit or no credit history, these amazing offers simply don't exist. We're living in a society that relies heavily on the need to have good credit and the habit of consumers to utilize credit in order to make purchases.

Unless you pay for absolutely everything you buy using cash, chances are, at least periodically you will utilize some form of credit. Credit is the process of borrowing money from a lender, then paying back what you owe over time, typically with interest. Most people have credit cards, one or more car loans, a mortgage, a home equity loan, student loans, and/or pay for big-ticket items (like major appliances, consumer electronics, or furniture) using credit offered by retail stores. Some credit is secured with your property or other assets used as collateral, whereas other credit, like credit cards, is unsecured (meaning no collateral is needed). Unsecured credit allows you to obtain credit based on your credit history. People use their credit cards to pay for everyday items, like gas, groceries, clothing, and meals. In fact, it's extremely difficult for people to exist in today's society without utilizing credit.

If you use credit cards and have various types of loans (such as a mortgage), you're certainly not alone. The United States Federal Reserve reports that as of late 2005, consumer debt was at $2.1 trillion. That's up from $1.7 trillion in 2001.

Take a look at some of these other credit and debt-related statistics:

- More than 185 million people in the United States have at least one credit card and the average interest for a credit card is 18.9 percent. What does it cost to utilize this credit? Well, if you pay only the minimum payment each month, it would take 25 years to pay off an $8,000 debt. Add the interest to the principal and you would ultimately pay over $24,000. (As you'll learn later in this book, there are ways to easily cut your credit card interest rates by shopping around for the best credit card deals. One place to find low interest credit card rates is the Lower My Bills web site, which can be found at www.lowermybills.com.)

- Approximately 46 percent of the U.S. population has at least two credit cards.
- It's estimated that 20 percent of Americans with credit cards have maxed out their lines of credit and that 25 percent of adults in the United States have a history of credit problems.
- The average amount of credit card debt in a typical U.S. household is $8,400.
- Approximately 24 percent of all personal expenditures in the United States are made using bank credit cards, retail cards, and debit cards.

Learning how to properly manage your credit and finances will help you protect your credit rating and credit score, which over time, will save you thousands or even tens of thousands of dollars. Information about your personal credit history is maintained and kept up-to-date (for creditors and lenders to access) on your credit report. Your credit report is compiled by three separate credit reporting agencies (also known as credit bureaus). You'll learn more about these organizations, which include Equifax, Experian, and TransUnion in later chapters.

Credit. When someone borrows money with the understanding it will be repaid, that person is given credit. Obtaining credit from a creditor has costs associated with it. The cost is incurred based on the interest rate and fees you'll be required to pay over time, in addition to the principal. Although the interest rate can be pre-set or variable, how much you ultimately pay will also be determined by the amount of time it takes you to fully repay the loan, whether it's a mortgage, credit card, car loan, or any other type of loan. As you'll learn from this book, there are many forms of loans and credit and each works slightly differently. Yet, any time you're granted credit by a creditor or lender, the information is recorded on your credit report and it impacts your credit score. TransUnion defines credit as, "A consumer's ability to make purchases, obtain services, or borrow money based on his or her promise, ability, and demonstrated willingness to repay."

Credit Rating. From a potential lender's standpoint, someone's credit rating is an estimate or educated guess relating to their credit worthiness—whether or not you'll repay your debt on time, with the appropriate interest. Your credit rating is a prediction regarding the likelihood of interest and capital actually being paid back and of the extent to which the lender is protected in the event of default. This numerical score (between 300 and 850) is calculated based on your credit (financial) reputation and history with creditors in the past.

Every time you apply for credit or a loan, the creditor or lender will check your *credit report* and *credit score*. Based on the information that's uncovered, you're either granted or approved for the credit or loan, or denied it. In many situations, the interest rates and fees you ultimately pay for the privilege of using credit are directly determined by your current credit worthiness, history, and credit score. People with a good credit history, who pay their bills on time, and who manage their finances and debt well, typically receive the best interest rates and lowest fees when they're granted credit. Negative information on your credit report typically means you're a credit risk. How much of a risk you are will help determine how much you ultimately pay for credit.

If you have an excellent credit rating and you apply for a $200,000, 30-year fixed rate mortgage, for example, you may be offered an interest rate of 6.25 percent. If, however, your credit rating is below average and there is negative information on your credit report, for that same mortgage you could be offered an interest rate of 8.5 percent or higher. The extra interest alone (between paying 6.25 percent and 8.5 percent) will be extremely significant over the 30-year period. The same rules apply on a car loan, student loan, home equity loan, credit cards, and other types of loans or credit.

Understanding how credit works, what information is incorporated into your credit report, and how your credit score is calculated will help you better manage your personal finances. This book is all about understanding how credit reports and credit scores work and discovering ways to ensure the information about you that potential creditors and lenders are given when you apply for credit or loans is accurate. As a consumer, you want your credit report and credit score to portray you in the best possible light, based on your credit worthiness.

Consider your credit report to be like your high school report card. Instead of listing each class, your credit report lists each creditor. As for your grades, your credit report lists your credit history and how responsible you've been with each creditor. The credit score you're given is like your grade point average. As a consumer, it's important to strive for a "B" or even an "A" average in order to be credit worthy and be able to receive the best credit offers and lowest interest rates. This translates to a credit score of over 650, but more on that later, in Chapter 2.

Credit Report. Compiled by one of the credit reporting agencies, such as Equifax, Experian, or TransUnion, a credit report contains personal and financial information about you, including your name, address, phone number, social security number, date of birth, past addresses, current and past employers, a listing of companies that have issued you credit (including credit cards, charge cards, car loans, mortgages, student loans, home equity loans, etc.), and details about your credit history (whether you pay your bills on time). Each of the major credit reporting agencies compiles a separate credit report for every individual. However, much of the information on each report should be identical or extremely similar.

Credit Reporting Agency (aka Credit Bureau). The three national bureaus that maintain credit reports on virtually all Americans with any type of credit history are Equifax, Experian, and TransUnion. These agencies maintain vast databases that are updated regularly. Their purpose is to supply creditors with timely and reliable financial information about individual consumers. It's important to understand that a credit reporting agency does not decide whether an individual qualifies for credit or not. Credit reporting agencies simply collect information that is relevant to a person's credit history and habits and then provides that information (for a fee), in the form of a credit report, to creditors and lenders. The three main credit reporting agencies also offer a variety of services to consumers designed to help people understand and manage their credit.

As you develop an understanding of what a credit report is and how it works, how your credit score is calculated, and the impact this information has on your ability to obtain credit, it becomes evident that it's absolutely critical that you pay your bills on time and that you manage your credit properly. Over extending yourself financially, making late payments, and not properly dealing with all of your creditors can have an extremely negative impact on your financial well-being and can hurt your chances of obtaining credit in the future.

As you'll learn, information that's listed on your credit report stays there for between seven and ten years (sometimes longer), depending on the type of information. Thus, defaulting on a loan, making late payments, or not paying your minimums on credit cards, for example, will have a long-term impact on your financial life. Although having incorrect information removed from your credit report is a straightforward process, having negative but accurate information deleted from your credit report is extremely difficult (and sometimes impossible), despite the ads you see from companies that offer "credit repair" services. Chapter 4 focuses on how to make corrections to your credit report.

Credit Score. Using a complex formula that's calculated based on many criteria related to your current financial situation and credit history, the three major credit reporting agencies calculate and regularly update your credit score. According to the Federal Trade Commission, "Most creditors use credit scoring to evaluate your credit record. This involves using your credit application and report to get information about you, such as your annual income, outstanding debt, bill paying history, and the number and types of accounts you have and how long you have had them. Potential lenders use your credit score to help predict whether you are a good risk to repay a loan and make payments on time." TransUnion reports someone's credit score is, "a mathematical calculation that reflects a consumer's creditworthiness. The score is an assessment of how likely a consumer is to pay his or her debts." Chapter 2 focuses exclusively on what a credit score is, how it's used, and how it's calculated.

What Is a Credit Report?

The three major credit reporting agencies maintain credit reports and credit scores on virtually everyone with a social security number and some type of credit history. That's over 170 million Americans. Someone's credit report becomes

TIP

There are many "credit repair" and "credit counseling" services that boast they can repair anyone's credit, regardless of what's in the credit history and what negative information is listed on the credit reports. This is simply untrue! As you'll discover, there are definitely legal and achievable ways to clean up your credit and boost your credit score, however, it's rarely a quick and easy process. Chapter 5 offers strategies on how to improve your credit report and boost your credit score legally, while Chapter 7 offers information about reputable resources you can utilize if you need help fixing your financial and credit problems.

active once they're granted credit, in the form of a credit card, charge card, student loan, or car loan, for example. Thus, many people begin to establish their credit histories around the age of 18 or in their early 20s. From that point forward, detailed and up-to-date personal and financial information is maintained by the credit reporting agencies and is made available to potential creditors and lenders in the form of a credit report. Every credit report gets updated monthly, based on new information provided by creditors.

Each of the credit reporting agencies maintains its own credit report for every individual. The information on the report is compiled from a variety of sources. According to

Experian, "Details about your financial behavior and identification information are contained in your personal credit report. This consumer-friendly report is sometimes called a credit file or a credit history. The typical consumer credit report includes four types of information. By law, we cannot disclose certain medical information (relating to physical, mental, or behavioral health or condition)."

TIP

Checking your credit report regularly (at least every three to six months) can help you prevent identity theft, and will allow you to better manage your personal financial situation. Before applying for credit, such as a mortgage, a car loan, or even a credit card, it's a good idea to review your credit report.

☆ ☆ **WARNING** ☆ ☆

The FBI reports that identity theft is currently the fastest growing crime in the United States. Often, criminals who steal people's identities utilize information from illegally obtained Social Security numbers and credit reports. One way to determine if you're a victim of identity theft is to check your credit reports regularly for irregularities. For example, look for credit cards that have been issued in your name, but that were never applied for or received by you. Also, check your credit card and bank account statements each month for transactions that don't belong to you. If you notice any problems, report them immediately to the appropriate financial institutions and law enforcement agencies. Identity theft can result in negative information being added to your credit report that doesn't belong to you. If not recognized and dealt with quickly, being an identity theft victim can lead to huge credit-related problems. Chapter 3 deals with preventing and identifying identity theft.

Information That's Included within Your Credit Report

Athough the format of your credit reports will vary, based on which credit reporting agency created it and how the report is obtained, the data is basically the same. The four main categories of information included on every credit report are described in the following sections.

Public Record Information

Public record information includes bankruptcy information and unpaid tax liens, for example, as well as details about civil law suits, judgments, and other legal proceedings recorded by a court. Bankruptcy information can remain on your credit report for up to 10 years. Unpaid tax liens can remain on the report for up to 15 years. Other public record information can remain on the report for up to seven years. In some states, this could also include overdue child support.

Credit Information

This includes details about all loans and credit you've been granted in the past. For each item, information on the report will include account specific details, such as the date opened, credit limit or loan amount, balance, monthly payment, and your payment pattern. The report also states whether anyone besides you (a joint account holder or cosigner, for example) is responsible for paying the account. Active positive credit information can remain on your report indefinitely, whereas most negative information in this category remains on your report for up to seven years.

Requests by Others to View Your Credit History

This section of your credit report will display details about who has received information from your credit report and who was given your name during the recent past, as allowed by law. According to the Fair Credit Reporting Act, credit grantors with a permissible purpose may inquire about your credit information *without* your prior consent. All inquires remain listed on your credit report for up to two years. Hard inquiries, which are the ones initiated with your permission when you apply for a credit card, loan, or mortgage, for example, will negatively impact your credit score for up to one year, although they'll remain listed on your report for two years.

Personal Information

This section of the credit report contains your personal details, including: your name, current and previous addresses, telephone number, your Social Security number, date of birth, and current and previous employers. Within the employment section of your credit report, information about your position (job title), and length of employment are listed for current and past jobs.

TIP

Information about your race, religious beliefs, medical history, personal lifestyle, political affiliation, friends, and your criminal record (if applicable) do *not* appear on your credit report and have no impact on your credit score. Other information that's *not* included on your credit report includes: checking or savings account balances, bankruptcies that are more than ten years old, and charged-off or debts placed for collection that are more than seven years old.

The Anatomy of Your Credit Report

Chapter 3 focuses on how to obtain a free copy of your credit report from each of the three major credit reporting agencies and will help you understand exactly what's listed on them, as well as the significance of that information. To quickly view the information listed on your credit report from all three of the major credit reporting agencies (Equifax, Experian, and TransUnion), be able to compare the information, and then check for inaccuracies, consider purchasing a comprehensive 3-in-1 credit report, which can be done online.

Whether you request copies of your credit reports through the mail or obtain the reports online, the information will be the same, although the data might be formatted differently on the page (or computer screen).

How the Information on Your Credit Report Is Compiled

Every month, every creditor and collection agency you're actively involved with will report details about you to one, two, or all three of the major credit reporting agencies. Your credit report and credit score will then be updated. Although it's possible that no new information will be added during any given month, older (preexisting) information remains on your credit report for between seven and ten years (sometimes longer). As you'll learn, this preexisting information will continue to impact your credit score for as long as it remains on your credit report.

TIP

Any creditor or lender you borrow money from has the ability to add information (positive or negative) to your credit report, as long as that information is current and accurate. Collection agencies that represent utilities (gas, electric, telephone service, cable TV, etc.); medical offices and hospitals; or any other type of company that you owe money to, can also add negative information to your credit report on their client's behalf, if you're late or negligent in paying, causing the account to be turned over to a collection agency.

☆ ☆ **WARNING** ☆ ☆

Many people don't realize that failure to pay a doctor's bill, for example, can eventually have a negative impact on your credit report and credit score, if that unpaid bill goes to collections. Likewise, although the utility companies or cell phone companies don't generally report to the credit reporting agencies, if a bill goes unpaid and gets transferred to a collection agency, that negative information will eventually appear on your credit report and could dramatically lower your credit score.

Who Can View My Credit Report?

According to the Office of the Attorney General of The United States, "Any business, individual, or government agency may request a credit report for its legitimate business needs involving a transaction with the consumer. Valid reasons for a company to review your credit report and credit score include: credit granting considerations; review or collection of an account; employment considerations; insurance underwriting; a potential partnership; security clearance; or lease. Reports may also be issued at the written request of the consumer or a court."

Some of the companies, individuals, and organizations that can obtain a copy of your credit report (in order to make a credit worthiness or business-related decision pertaining to you) include:

- A company you hire to monitor your credit report for signs of identity theft
- Any government agency
- Any state or local child support enforcement agency
- Anyone who has your written authorization to obtain your credit report
- Current or potential landlords
- Employers and potential employers
- Groups considering your application for a government license or benefit
- Insurance companies

> **TIP**
>
> Certain types of inquiries that don't involve you applying for new credit or a loan are called "soft inquiries." Although these are listed on your credit report, they do not impact your credit score. A "soft inquiry" might come from a potential landlord, a government agency, or a credit card company or mortgage broker doing market research without your knowledge to "pre-qualify" you as a cardholder or potential lender.

- Potential lenders (credit card companies, mortgage brokers, car dealerships, banks, financial institutions, etc.)
- Someone who uses your credit report to provide a product or service you have requested

Why Your Credit Report Is so Important

When you apply for a job; attempt to make a purchase using credit; buy a home or rent an apartment; attempt to purchase or lease a car; apply for a student loan (for yourself or your children); apply for a credit or charge card; open a checking account with overdraft protection at a bank or financial institution; or apply for a new insurance policy, your credit report and credit score will be evaluated. What someone finds listed on your credit report will directly impact your ability to make a purchase using credit or obtain a loan. Any company that's allowed to obtain and evaluate a copy of your credit report can accomplish this in a matter of minutes and then make quick, but intelligent business decisions based on your credit score.

Throughout this book, you'll find dozens of tips for properly managing information on your credit report, strategies for how to effectively deal with creditors (and collection agencies), steps to follow in order to maintain the highest possible credit score, and information you need to save money on interest rates and fees associated with utilizing credit. Because the information contained within your credit report is so important when it comes to obtaining credit and loans, it's vital that you take the steps necessary to insure the information on your credit report created by each of the three major credit reporting agencies is up-to-date and accurate. Furthermore, because having and being able to utilize credit has become such an important part of our culture, it's more vital than ever that as a consumer, you take steps to insure the information reported to the credit reporting agencies by your creditors and lenders is positive.

The easiest way to ensure the information listed on your credit report is positive (which will help boost your credit score) is simply to pay your bills on time on a monthly basis and to immediately begin paying off any old debt that's been negatively listed on your credit report. As you'll discover, there are also many other things you can do to improve your credit rating over time.

One important thing to remember when it comes to your credit report and credit score is that negative information (such as a late or skipped credit card or loan payment) will immediately have a negative impact on your credit score. However, "repairing" that negative information could take months or years.

Many people who apply for a mortgage, attempt to refinance a mortgage, apply for a car loan, or who apply for a credit card, for example, are often surprised to learn that their credit score (and their credit worthiness) has dropped considerably due to recent late or missed payments. As you'll learn, even one late mortgage payment over a two- or three-year period will hamper your ability to obtain the best interest rate and overall deal

---

TIP

Many Americans run into financial problems at various times in their lives. This is common. Instead of ignoring bills and skipping payments, however, it's important to at least make timely minimum monthly payments and stay in touch with your creditors, keeping them apprised of your financial situation if a problem arises. If you can't meet your financial obligations for a few months, your creditors and lenders will often work with you if you show good faith, stay in contact, and are cooperative with them.

---

when you attempt to refinance your mortgage or apply for a new mortgage if you're planning to move, for example.

Once you understand the importance of your credit report and credit score, it's important to carefully analyze your current financial situation, then do whatever you can to improve or remove any negative information that could impact your ability to obtain credit in the future. This is particularly important if your future plans involve applying for a mortgage, a car loan, a home equity loan, a credit card, a student loan, or some other type of loan for a major purchase. Never wait until the last minute to begin addressing problems with your credit report because fixing inaccuracies or having the report updated after overdue payments are made can take 30 to 90 days (sometimes longer).

> **TIP**
>
> If you're planning to apply for a mortgage, home equity loan, car loan, student loan, or make some other type of significant purchase using credit, be sure to read Chapters 5 and 6 carefully.

Now that you understand the relevance of your credit report and credit score on your financial well-being, Chapter 2 focuses specifically on understanding the significance of your credit score and how it's calculated.

Solving Credit
Score Mysteries

WHAT'S IN THIS CHAPTER

➢ What is a credit score?

➢ How your credit score is calculated.

➢ The difference between a "credit score" and a "FICO® score."

➢ The impact your credit score has on your financial life.

➢ The inside scoop on FICO Scores from the company that calculates them.

What Is a Credit Score?

Your credit score is a three-digit number that is an indicator of your credit worthiness. In other words, it's a tool that helps a creditor or lender gauge its risk level if you are approved for a loan or granted credit.

The information on your credit report includes detailed information about your existing credit, your payment history, and other pertinent data a creditor can use to make intelligent decisions about whether or not to grant you credit or some type of loan. In the past, for a creditor to make this decision, it would require a person with specialized training to carefully analyze all of the information on someone's credit report manually, then make a determination about their credit worthiness. That was how things were done about two decades ago. Today, thanks to computers, the process is far more automated and decisions can be made in seconds, not hours or days, thanks to the introduction of credit scoring.

Using only information that's found on your credit report, a complex mathematical algorithm is used to calculate a credit score based on a variety of criteria, each of which is weighted differently. The result is a number, between 300 and 850, that represents how much of a credit risk you are as a consumer.

A credit score in the 300s or 400s is given to someone who has a history of being an extremely high credit risk, while a score in the mid-600s to low-700s is considered a good credit risk. Someone with a credit score in the mid-to-high 700s or in the 800s is considered an excellent credit risk. These are the people who get the best deals in terms of low interest rates, for example, when applying for loans and credit cards.

It's important to remember that different lenders and creditors give different weight to these scores. When making their decisions to approve a loan or credit, the following table displays how credit scores and FICO Scores are generally perceived by lenders and creditors.

Excellent	Over 750
Very good	721 or higher
Acceptable (average)	661 to 720
Uncertain	620 to 660
High risk	Less than 619

Each of the credit reporting agencies (Experian, Equifax, and TransUnion) maintains a separate credit report on every consumer. In conjunction with this credit report, each has a corresponding credit score. The information on each credit report is often slightly different because not all creditors report data to all three credit bureaus. Thus, when you review your three credit reports side-by-side, you'll often notice small discrepancies (which is normal). Because your credit score is calculated by the data on each credit report, each of your credit scores will also be slightly different.

When you apply for a major credit card or store credit card, for example, that creditor will check your credit history by reviewing your credit report obtained from one of the credit reporting agencies. Which agency they use (Experian, Equifax, or TransUnion) is their decision. In many cases, when you're offered a credit decision in under five minutes, that decision was based exclusively on your credit score that went along with the credit report accessed. The quick approval or rejection was an automated decision.

When you apply for a more substantial loan, such as a mortgage, the mortgage broker or mortgage finance company will typically access all three of your credit reports, then use the middle credit score as a tool to help make an approval decision. If only two credit scores are available, which is not unusual, then the mortgage company will rely on the lower of the two credit scores.

Because the information on your credit report constantly changes, as creditors report new or updated data, and old data (over seven years old) drops off your credit report, your credit score from each credit reporting agencies also changes. The information, however, is based exclusively on information found in that credit report. In other words, your credit score does *not* take the following data into account:

- Personal information, such as your sex, race, religion, nationality, or sexual orientation
- Your checking or savings account balances
- The value of your personal assets

Your credit score is a tool that creditors and lenders use to quickly and objectively measure your level of credit risk, because this score represents the likelihood that you'll repay your debt on time. Because this score is considered an extremely reliable indication of someone's credit worthiness, is can be used to make automated decisions quickly. A creditor or lender can obtain your credit score in a matter of seconds, then often make a loan or credit approval decision in just minutes, which is something that could not have been done before, without the use of credit scores as a decision-making tool.

Because credit scores are calculated by a computer using only information that appears within your credit report, there is little or no room for human biases in the decision-making process. Thus, it's much harder for a lender or creditor to discriminate against someone based on their gender, race, religion, nationality, marital status, or sexual orientation.

In today's world, your credit score carries a lot of weight. Not only do creditors use it to make decisions, this data is also used by insurance companies when issuing new policies. Employers can use information from your credit report and your credit score to help with hiring decisions, and landlords often use this data to help determine how responsible a potential tenant will be.

Your credit score is an important number that needs to be protected by you as a consumer. Making irresponsible or bad financial decisions, making late payments, applying for too much credit, and a variety of other factors can all work against you and dramatically lower your credit score. Remember, not

TIP

Be sure to read Chapters 4 and 5 for detailed information
about how to protect and improve your credit score.

only will your credit score help to determine whether you're
granted credit or a loan, it will also directly help to determine
what interest rate and fees you ultimately pay when using
credit or taking out a loan. Having a below-average credit
score will cost you a lot of money now and in the future,
because you will be paying much higher interest rates than
someone with excellent credit.

$E = MC^2$ Is a Complex Formula . . .
Your Credit Score May Seem Just as Complex

Your credit score is not an arbitrary number. It's a numerical
score that's based on data from your credit report that is evaluated using a complex and periodically changed mathematical algorithm. Each of the three credit reporting agencies
(credit bureaus) uses its own version of this formula, although
the final score you earn will carry equal weight, no matter
which credit reporting agency it comes from.

Using a proprietary mathematical formula that is modified
as consumer trends change, your credit score is calculated
based on the following criteria:

- *Your payment history.* This takes into account your payment information on specific types of loans, including your mortgage, auto loan, credit cards, retail accounts, and so on. It also takes into account any negative information listed in the public records section of your credit report, such as a bankruptcy, judgments, law suits, liens, wage attachments, collection items, and so on. Within the calculation, not only is your score impacted based on how many late payments you have listed on your credit report, but the amount past due and how late the payment(s) are is also factored into the equation. On the positive side, your credit score will get a boost for each current account that's listed as "paid as agreed."

- *The amounts you owe.* This takes into account the amount of money you owe on accounts, the types of accounts, the number of accounts you have with balances, the portion of each credit line used, and the portion of installment loan amounts still owing.

- *The length of your credit history.* This refers to the time since each account was first opened and the amount of time that has passed since the last activity on the account.

- *New credit.* The number of newly opened accounts, the number of recent credit inquiries, the time that's passed since your last new accounts were opened, and the time since the most recent inquiries were made are all taken into account.

TIP

Your payment history and amounts owned represent about 65 percent of what comprises your FICO Score.

- *Types of credit used.* The number and types of accounts listed on your credit report all play a role in the calculation of your credit score. The number of accounts will include the number of car loans, mortgages, and credit cards.

All of this information is taken into account as your credit score or FICO Score is calculated. Depending on your overall credit profile, the amount of weight each piece of information or data is given will vary dramatically from person to person; however, your positive or negative payment history is typically weighted the heaviest when the credit score calculation is made. Thus, late payments and other negative information will lower your score, while maintaining or re-establishing a positive track record over time (in terms of timely payments) will boost your score.

Credit Score versus FICO Score: What's the Difference?

Here's where things get a little confusing. Fair Isaac Corporation is the company that first created credit scores, called FICO Scores. These scores are used by all three credit reporting agencies, as well as over 70 percent of all creditors and lenders. Thus, it's your FICO Score that's important. However, how that FICO Score is calculated by each of the three credit bureaus is slightly different, although all three will range between 300 and 850. You'll know if you're looking at your genuine FICO Score only if it's labeled "Officially Certified FICO Credit Score."

Each of the three credit reporting agencies as well as certain creditors also calculate their own version of each consumer's credit score that's based on information on your credit report. These scores are simply called "Credit Scores," which may or may not be the actual score lenders and creditors use to make their decisions.

TIP

When you request a copy of your credit report and credit score, make sure the credit score you receive is your genuine FICO Score, not a different number calculated by a company other than Fair Isaac Corporation. Although a different number will give you a ballpark figure in regard to what the lenders and creditors may be looking at, your genuine FICO Score offers the most accurate representation of your credit worthiness, based on information the lenders and creditors will actually be using.

To determine your actual FICO Score and be able to monitor it on an ongoing basis, you can purchase this information from Fair Isaac Corporation's web site (www.myfico.com). For example, for $7.95 per month (or one annual payment of $79.95), you can subscribe to the Score Watch service offered at MyFICO.com. This service provides continuous monitoring of your Equifax Credit Report and FICO Score, notifies you when you may qualify for better interest rates, e-mails you when changes to your FICO Score or credit report are detected, and how key positive and negative factors are impacting your personal score, based on information that is in your credit report.

The FICO Standard ($14.95) and FICO Deluxe ($44.85) services both include access to your credit reports and FICO Scores, and provides access to the proprietary FICO Simulator, which will help you better calculate your FICO Score based on hypothetical scenarios, like if you were to pay off debts, add new accounts, or make late payments.

TIP

To see firsthand how much you could be saving on your current and future credit needs based on potential improvements or drops in your credit score and current interest rates, check out MyFICO.com's Loan Savings Calculator. It's a free online tool available at www.myfico.com/myfico/CreditCentral/Loan Rates.asp#Calculator.

What's a VantageScore?

As if the whole credit score thing weren't complicated enough, in early 2006, yet another credit scoring system was implemented. This system is designed to make the credit scores provided by the three credit reporting agencies more uniform for each consumer. Plus, to make the score easier to understand, it is accompanied by a letter grade (ranging from "A" to "F").

Until now, the information on a typical consumer's three credit reports varied, which translated to sometimes vastly different credit scores corresponding with each report. This new system is reported to reduce the discrepancy between scores by up to 30 percent. In order to calculate this new VantageScore, the participating credit reporting agencies use a single methodology, as opposed to three slightly different formulas.

The new VantageScore calculates credit scores based on a range between 501 and 990. Like the FICO Score system (which uses a range of 300 to 850), the higher your score, the better. The corresponding letter grades associated with each VantageScore are as follows:

- 501 to 600 = "F" (very poor credit)
- 601 to 700 = "D"
- 701 to 800 = "C"
- 801 to 900 = "B"
- 901 to 990 = "A" (excellent credit)

Although the new VantageScore was made available to mortgage lenders, banks, and credit card companies starting in March 2006, consumers weren't granted access to their new scores until late 2006. Because so many lenders have been using the FICO Score model and making decisions based on three available scores (from the three credit reporting agencies), it's yet to be seen whether or not this new system will be widely adopted and if it is, how quickly the transition will take place. The VantageScore system could someday replace the FICO Score system if it gets widely adopted and used by creditors and lenders. However, the transition could take years, perhaps decades.

Because the new system uses a broader range, many consumers may immediately see their credit scores rise. However, there rises probably won't increase their chances of getting approved for loans or credit because the scores are being weighted differently by the lenders and creditors.

TIP

At the time this book was written, the three credit reporting agencies hadn't yet decided how they'd make the new VantageScore available to consumers, or whether consumers would be charged for the information.

The Inside Scoop on FICO Scores from the Company that Calculates Them

Craig Watts is the public affairs manager for Fair Isaac Corporation, the company that originally created the FICO Score system that's so widely used today. In this interview, Watts explains more about FICO Scores and how to improve your score using easy-to-follow strategies and advice.

Fair Isaac Corporation (NYSE: FIC) is the leading provider of credit scoring, decision management, fraud detection, and credit risk score services. Thousands of companies in more than 60 countries use Fair Isaac technology to acquire customers more efficiently, increase customer value and retention, reduce fraud and credit losses, lower operating costs, and enter new markets more profitably.

The company was founded in 1956 on the premise that data, used intelligently, can improve business decisions. Today, the company's solutions, software, and consulting services power more than 180 billion smarter business decisions each year for companies worldwide.

Most leading banks and credit card issuers rely on Fair Isaac solutions, as do insurers, retailers, telecommunications providers, healthcare organizations, and government agencies. Through the www.MyFICO.com web site, consumers use the company's FICO Scores, the standard measure of credit risk, to manage their financial well-being.

When did FICO Scores first get introduced in America?

Craig: Automated credit reports were made available for the first time in the late 1970s. Using automated credit reports, the company developed the algorithm that calculates FICO Scores. The system was introduced in 1989 by Equifax. Our formula to calculate FICO Scores is now part of the operating system used by all three credit reporting agencies. Over 70 percent of all lenders and creditors rely on FICO Scores to help them make their lending or credit granting decisions. The three credit reporting agencies also calculate their own credit scores, plus many lenders and creditors have their own algorithms for calculating credit scores that are used inhouse. FICO Scores are the only scores, however, that are widely used by lenders and that are available to consumers.

How is someone's FICO Score actually calculated?

Craig: There is a mathematical algorithm that we've created that's made available to the three credit reporting agencies in the form of software. This formula is modified somewhat every few years, based on new or evolving trends. Each algorithm used by the credit reporting agencies is also slightly different. Since 1989, we have never stopped redeveloping the algorithm that's used to calculate FICO Scores. The three credit reporting agencies do not cooperate. In fact, they compete extremely heavily against each other. Each of these agencies uses our credit scoring system to give themselves a competitive edge.

What are some of the recent trends used to calculate FICO Scores?

Craig: When Fair Isaac Corporation first developed the FICO Score system in the late 1980s, our research indicated that when people shopped around for car loans or mortgages, for example, they didn't have a lot of options, so they spent only about one week shopping for their best deals before making a decision. When we determined that people shopped for seven days, we modified the formula so that it ignored multiple inquiries from mortgage or car loan lenders within a seven day period and counted them as just one inquiry.

Over the years, our research has shown that people have begun spending more time researching and shopping around for their best options for mortgages and car loans. Thus, over the years, this seven day window was expanded to 14 days in the late 1990s. It was later expanded again to 30 days. Most recently, we've expanded the window to 45 days, during which time someone can have multiple inquiries from a mortgage or car loan lender count as just one inquiry on their credit report.

Another significant change to the way the score is calculated happened recently. In the past, if someone sought out credit counseling and it was reflected on their credit report, their credit score was negatively impacted. This is no longer the case. We now encourage people to seek out credit counseling when it's needed. This will have no impact on their FICO Score.

Inquiries from lenders detract from someone's credit score. How long does inquiry information remain listed on a credit report and how much of a negative impact does it have?

Craig: Hard inquiries remain on credit reports for two years. However, in terms of our FICO Score calculation, we only look at the number and types of inquiries over the previous 12 month period.

For a long time, people were told to close unused credit accounts in order to improve their credit scores. Is this still the case?

Craig: The credit score looks at your available credit and the amount you owe. From this data, your credit utilization rate is calculated. The credit utilization rate determines how close you are to maxing out your credit accounts as a whole. Those unused accounts contribute to the total amount of credit you have available. If you were to close those unused accounts, your total amount of available credit would immediately decrease, but your current credit balances would remain the same, since you've done nothing to pay them down. With the lower available credit, the formula would raise your credit utilization rate, which would be detrimental to your credit score. This is why closing unused credit accounts with zero balances can hurt you.

What can someone do to improve their FICO Score?

Craig: The most obvious and common sense answer is to always pay your bills on time. Never become late. The more late payments you have beyond 30-days, the worse off you'll be. If you have otherwise good credit, and one or two late payments suddenly appear on your credit report, that could cause your FICO Score to drop 50 to 100 points almost instantly. The higher your score is to begin with, the farther your score will tumble when negative information appears on your credit report. Just like your personal or professional reputation, it takes much longer to recover your credit score than it does to hurt it.

If your credit score has experienced a drop, what can be done to boost it up again?

Craig: The best thing you can do is get caught up with all of your creditors and then begin to once again pay all of your bills on time. If you're able to do this, you'll notice your FICO Score will gradually rise. We've seen people with bankruptcies listed on their credit reports receive credit or be approved for a prime-rate loans after three or four years of rebuilding their credit. That bankruptcy, however, will remain listed on the credit report for ten years.

What can someone do to quickly boost their FICO Score?

Craig: Make sure your account balances on revolving accounts, such as credit cards, remains low compared to your credit limits. This will improve your score. Paying down your credit card debt will help your score, plus save you money. Ideally, you want to keep each credit card balance under 35 percent of your current limit. For the best impact on your credit score, pay off your credit card debt to zero.

The reason why it's difficult to quickly raise your FICO Score is because this number is supposed to represent your credit reputation. If you have a history of being a credit risk, you need to show improvement over time in order to be rewarded with a higher credit score.

The FICO Score is a summary of your entire credit history, not just what's happened in the past few weeks or months. If your score has dropped below 500, for example, it didn't happen by accident. The low score is a result of your ongoing actions when it comes to managing your debt, finances, and credit.

One thing you can do to quickly improve your score, however, is to correct any errors on your credit report that could be keeping your score down. Corrections can be made in as little as 10 to 30 days, assuming the corrections you're seeking are legitimate. You can not have accurate information that is negative removed from your credit report simply by initiating a dispute. When someone has a credit score over 800, it's because they've demonstrated good credit habits over many years.

What is the bare minimum credit score someone should aim for in order to get good deals on loans and credit?

Craig: That's a difficult question, because every lender and creditor has its own criteria for approving loans or granting credit. Some lenders are very risk adverse. Other lenders are much more willing to advance credit to higher risk borrowers. Asking this question is like asking what's the ideal SAT score to achieve in order to get into college. The answer is that every college and university has its own criteria for what it looks for.

As a general rule, within the mortgage industry, having a FICO Score of 700 or above will allow you to qualify for the best prime-rate loans.

TIP

By visiting the MyFICO.com web site and clicking on the "Loan Center" icon, based on where you live and your current FICO Score, you can review a list of lenders in your region that will accept you for various types of credit or loans. You can also review current interest rates for loans, based on what you potentially qualify for.

Why is someone's FICO Score different from each credit reporting agency, even of the three reports were accessed at the same time?

Craig: There are three reasons for this. First, different information is reported to different credit reporting agencies. For example, a mortgage or credit card company may only report data to one or two, not all three of the credit bureaus and this will impact your score. Also, the algorithm used to calculate someone's FICO Score is slightly different with each credit reporting agency. Finally, the three credit reporting agencies have different search capabilities for finding and listing information in the Public Records section of the credit report, which also impacts your credit score.

In your opinion, is there a reason why the new VantageScore system won't work?

Craig: Unless all three of the credit reporting agencies start pooling and sharing their data and stop being so competitive with one another, the ability to calculate one true credit score that applies to all three credit reports is unlikely to happen. The mortgage industry has relied on using what are called 'merged credit reports' for almost 20 years. This is a compilation of data from all three credit reporting agencies that's similar to three-in-one credit reports available to consumers. It remains unknown whether lenders will adopt this new credit scoring system and change the way they currently make their lending decisions. Time will determine if the VantageScore system is actually a good measure of credit risk and someone's credit worthiness. The proof will be in the pudding.

What are some of the biggest misconceptions people have about FICO Scores?

Craig: One of the biggest misconceptions is that the FICO Score system takes into account someone's income and assets. This isn't true at all. The score is based on how you've handled credit in the past, not how much money you have in your checking or savings account, for example. I have seen people at the poverty level have excellent credit scores, and multi-millionaires have very low credit scores, because they paid their bills late, and were not responsible with their credit or managing their loans.

Another misconception is that creditors and lenders use someone's FICO Score exclusively to make decisions. This too is often false. Many creditors use someone's credit score as one tool. When you apply for a mortgage, for example, someone will evaluate all of the information actually listed on your credit report, check your credit score, and inquire about things like your employment history and your earning history before making a decision.

One of the only times when a FICO Score alone is used to grant credit is when you apply for instant credit at a department store or retail store, or a financial institution offers instant approval for a credit card. In this case, a computer will look up your FICO Score and make a decision using a fully automated process. If you're not immediately accepted, however, you can then complete a full credit application and have it reviewed. Credit scores are also used by credit card companies to provide pre-approved credit card offers to select groups of consumers who fit a specific credit profile.

Why don't the credit reporting agencies automatically provide a FICO Score when someone requests their annual free credit report?

Craig: This is a business decision made by the credit reporting agencies. The Fair Credit Reporting Act requires the credit reporting agencies to supply consumers with free copies of their credit reports upon request once every 12 months. Until this law was passed, the consumer had to pay for this information. Because the credit score is not actually part of the credit report, this is a piece of information that credit reporting agencies can still charge extra for. If you are supplied with a credit score, it's important to determine if it's a score that creditors and lenders actually use.

How can a consumer know if they're receiving the right credit score?

Craig: There is only one credit score used by the majority of lenders and creditors that is also available to consumers and that's the FICO Score. If the score doesn't say it's a genuine FICO Score when a consumer sees it, chances are it's some other type of score that the lenders and creditors aren't actually using to make their decisions. Equifax is the only credit reporting agency that automatically supplies consumers with their FICO Score when they purchase their credit score information in addition to their credit report from one of the credit reporting agencies. The MyFICO.com web site is another resource for purchasing your actual FICO Score. Again, this is the score that the majority of lenders and creditors are actually using. It's not what we call an imitation score. If you want to be 98 percent sure you're looking at the same data as creditors and lenders, request your credit reports directly from the credit bureaus, then obtain your genuine FICO Score from the MyFICO.com web site.

Where to Go from Here

Now that you have a basic understanding of what your credit report is and the information it contains, and you realize the importance of your credit score and the impact it has on your financial life, it's important to take this information and begin applying it to your day-to-day money and credit management practices.

Chapter 3 explains how to obtain copies of your credit reports from the three credit reporting agencies. In subsequent chapters, you'll discover how to make corrections to your credit report, establish, maintain, or rebuild your credit, and learn additional ways to improve your credit score.

Obtaining Your
Credit Report
and Credit Score

WHAT'S IN THIS CHAPTER

➤ How to request a copy of your credit report from each of the three credit reporting agencies.

➤ The benefits of purchasing a three-in-one credit report with your credit scores.

➤ Understanding what's on your credit report.

➤ Preventing identity theft: Why it's important to monitor your credit report over time.

How to Request Free Copies of Your Credit Report Annually

As you know, there are three independent credit reporting agencies—Equifax, Experian, and TransUnion. Thus, it's necessary to request your credit report from each of them. Then, if corrections need to be made, it's necessary to contact each credit reporting agency separately. In addition to your credit report, your unique credit score is available for a small fee. Your credit report is available for free from each credit reporting agency once every 12 months.

An alternative to requesting individual credit reports from each credit reporting agency is to obtain a comprehensive three-in-one credit report. This is a single report that compiles data from all three credit reporting agencies (and in many cases, includes your credit score from each bureau). It's necessary to purchase a three-in-one credit report or subscribe to a credit monitoring service.

There are three ways to obtain a free copy of your credit report. As you'll discover, the fastest and easiest method is to initiate the request online. In less than five minutes, you can be viewing a copy of your credit report on your computer screen (or print out the information in an easy-to-read format).

If you don't have access to the internet, you can request a copy of your credit report by completing a single-page Annual Credit Report Request Form or by sending a letter to The Annual Credit Report Request Service. You can also call one toll-free number to have copies of your credit report mailed to you.

☆ ☆ **WARNING** ☆ ☆

When you request a free copy of your credit report, it will not include your credit score. For a small fee (under $6), you can request your corresponding credit score from each credit reporting agency when you receive your free report. When obtaining your credit score, be sure it's a genuine FICO Score.

Submitting Your Request by Mail

Once every 12 months, you can request a free copy of your credit report from each of the credit reporting agencies by completing the Annual Credit Report Request Form (see Figure 3.1). The form is available from www.annualcreditre port.com or www.ftc.gov/credit.

The Annual Credit Report Request Service is sponsored by all three credit reporting agencies and authorized by the Federal Trade Commission. It allows you to request one, two, or all three of your credit reports with a single request. This can be done by mail, phone, or via the internet.

To complete the one-page Annual Credit Report Request Form, you'll need to provide the following information:

- Social Security number
- Date of birth
- First name

FIGURE 3.1: **ANNUAL CREDIT REPORT**

EQUIFAX   **experian**   **TransUnion.**

Annual Credit Report Request Form

You have the right to get a free copy of your credit file disclosure, commonly called a credit report, once every 12 months, from each of the nationwide consumer credit reporting companies - Equifax, Experian and TransUnion.

For instant access to your free credit report, visit www.annualcreditreport.com.

For more information on obtaining your free credit report, visit www.annualcreditreport.com or call 877-322-8228.

Use this form if you prefer to write to request your credit report from any, or all, of the nationwide consumer credit reporting companies. The following information is required to process your request. **Omission of any information may delay your request.**

Once complete, fold (do not staple or tape), place into a #10 envelope, affix required postage and mail to:
Annual Credit Report Request Service P.O. Box 105281 Atlanta, GA 30348-5281.

Please use a Black or Blue Pen and write your responses in PRINTED CAPITAL LETTERS without touching the sides of the boxes like the examples listed below:

A B C D E F G H I J K L M N O P Q R S T U V W X Y Z   0 1 2 3 4 5 6 7 8 9

Social Security Number:

Date of Birth:
Month / Day / Year

- - - - - - Fold Here - - - - - -   - - - - - - Fold Here - - - - - -

First Name   **M.I.**

Last Name   JR, SR, III, etc.

Current Mailing Address:

House Number   Street Name

Apartment Number / Private Mailbox   **For Puerto Rico Only: Print Urbanization Name**

City   **State**   **ZipCode**

Previous Mailing Address (complete only if at current mailing address for less than two years):

House Number   Street Name

- - - - - - Fold Here - - - - - -   - - - - - - Fold Here - - - - - -

Apartment Number / Private Mailbox   **For Puerto Rico Only: Print Urbanization Name**

City   **State**   **ZipCode**

Shade Circle Like This → ●

Not Like This → ⊗ ⌀

I want a credit report from (shade each that you would like to receive):
○ Equifax
○ Experian
○ TransUnion

○ Shade here if, for security reasons, you want your credit report to include no more than the last four digits of your Social Security Number.

If additional information is needed to process your request, the consumer credit reporting company will contact you by mail.

Your request will be processed within 15 days of receipt and then mailed to you.

Copyright 2004, Central Source LLC

31238

- Middle initial
- Last name
- Current address (If you've lived at your address for less than two years, you'll also need to provide your complete previous address.)
- At the bottom of the Annual Credit Report Request Form, you must request your credit report from each of the credit reporting agencies, or state specifically which report(s) you're interested in receiving.

To complete the written form, be sure to use black or blue ink and write in clear, block letters. *All* of the requested information must be provided to process your request. An alternative to completing the Annual Credit Report Request Form is to write a letter, addressed to the Annual Credit Report Request Service, containing all of the previously listed information.

The completed form or your letter should be sent in a standard #10 envelope to Annual Credit Report Request Service, P.O. Box 105281, Atlanta, GA 30348-5281.

TIP

Requesting copies of your credit report by mail will take 15 days to be processed, plus additional time for the reports to be mailed to you.

☆ ☆ **WARNING** ☆ ☆

Many companies will advertise an offer to provide a free copy of your credit report, however, to obtain the free report, you often need to subscribe to a credit monitoring service or purchase some other item or product. To obtain a truly free copy of your credit report with no strings attached, The Annual Credit Report Request Service is the only service authorized by The Federal Trade Commission (FTC). Beware of impostors and other companies that look or sound official.

According to the FTC,

Under federal law, you're entitled to an additional free report if a company takes adverse action against you such as denying your application for credit, insurance, or employment and you ask for your report within 60 days of receiving notice of the action. The notice will give you the name, address, and phone number of the consumer reporting company. You're also entitled to one free report a year if you're unemployed and plan to look for a job within 60 days; if you're on welfare; or if your report is inaccurate because of fraud, including identity theft. Otherwise, a consumer reporting company may charge you up to $9.50 for another copy of your report within a 12-month period.

Requesting Your Free Credit Report by Telephone

By calling the Annual Credit Report Request Service toll-free at (877) 322-8228, you can follow the automated voice prompts and request copies of your credit report from each of the three credit reporting agencies be mailed to you within 15 days. When placing this call, be prepared to provide your telephone number, social security number, date of birth, full name, and address. If you've lived at your current address for less than two years, you'll need to provide your previous address as well.

Obtaining Your Credit Report Online

Using a computer that's connected to the internet, you can request and obtain a copy of your credit report from each of the three credit reporting agencies in under five minutes. Point your web browser to the official Annual Credit Report Request Service's web site (www.AnnualCreditReport .com), select your home state, and complete the brief online form (see Figure 3.2).

You'll be asked to provide your full name, date of birth, Social Security number, and current address. If you've lived at your current address for less than two years, you'll also be asked for your previous address. At the bottom of the on-screen questionnaire, you'll see a security code in a multi-colored box. At the appropriate prompt, reenter this security code and click the "Next" icon to continue.

You will now be prompted to select one or more of the nationwide consumer credit reporting companies to request your free credit report from. Using your mouse, place an

FIGURE 3.2: ANNUAL CREDIT REPORT WEB SITE

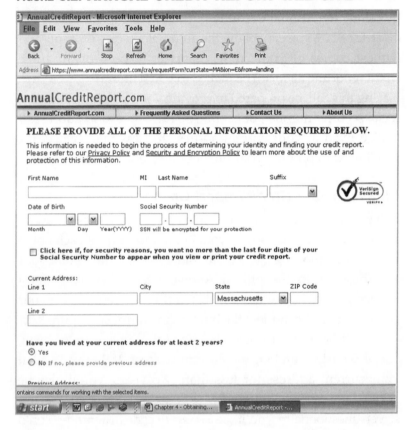

on-screen check mark next to one, two, or all three of the available options, which include Experian, Equifax, and TransUnion (see Figure 3.3). When you've checked the desired options, click on the "Next" icon located in the lower-right corner of the screen.

FIGURE 3.2: **ANNUAL CREDIT REPORT WEB SITE**

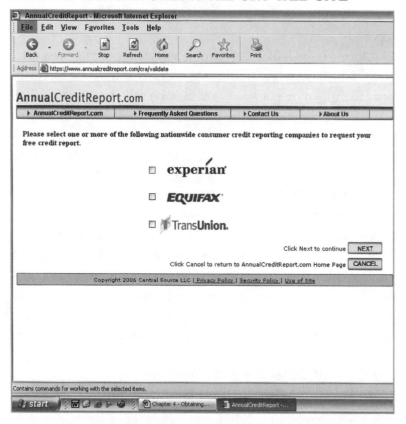

At this point, you will be transferred to the official web site of each credit reporting agency, one at a time, to obtain your free credit report. Once you've obtained each report and printed it out, click on the "Return to AnnualCreditReport.com" icon at the top of the screen to return to the AnnualCredit

Report.com web site. You'll then be re-directed the web site of another credit reporting agency, if you've requested multiple reports.

Once you're at each credit reporting agency's web site, you'll be asked a few additional security questions to verify your identity. For example, you may be asked a question like, "According to your credit profile, you may have opened a mortgage loan in or around [insert month and year]. Please select the lender to whom you currently make your mortgage payments. If you do not have a mortgage, select 'NONE OF THE ABOVE/DOES NOT APPLY.'" You'll then be provided with four or five possible options to choose from. Be prepared to answer three to five different security questions when visiting each of the credit reporting agency's web sites as part of your credit report request. Upon answering the security questions correctly, your credit report will promptly be displayed on the computer screen. Choose the "Print Your Report" option to view a printer-friendly version of your credit report.

The Cost of Obtaining Additional or More Frequent Credit Reports

If you want to obtain copies of your credit report more frequently than once every 12 months, there are several ways to do this. You can purchase single copies of your report from each of the credit reporting agencies, or you can subscribe to a credit monitoring service which includes unlimited access to your credit report (and potentially your credit score) for a monthly fee.

For a fee of up to $9.50 each, to purchase single copies of your credit report from each of the three credit reporting agencies, contact them directly:

- Equifax, (800) 685-1111, www.equifax.com
- Experian, (888) 397-3742, www.experian.com
- TransUnion, (800) 916-8800, www.transunion.com

The consumer division of each of these credit reporting agencies also offer online credit monitoring services and the ability to purchase copies of your credit report with a corresponding credit score. For an additional fee, you can also obtain a three-in-one credit report (listing information from all three credit reporting agencies on one report). Some of these three-in-one reports also include your credit scores.

What about Your Credit Score?

As you learned in Chapter 2, in addition to the credit report that's compiled by each of the three credit reporting agencies (aka credit bureaus), each also calculates your credit score. This is the number that many creditors use to quickly make decisions about whether or not to grant you credit or approve a loan.

Although you're entitled to a free copy of your credit report every 12 months, the credit reporting agencies are not obligated to provide you with your credit score for free. Instead, they charge you to obtain it. At the time you request a free copy of your credit report, you may receive an offer to purchase your corresponding credit score and receive the

TIP

Your credit score is sometimes referred to as your FICO Score. FICO is a registered trademark of Fair Isaac Corporation (NYSE:FIC), the pioneer of the FICO credit score that's used by many lenders to evaluate consumer credit risk. According to the company's web site, "Credit reporting agency risk scores produced from models developed by Fair Isaac Corporation are commonly known as FICO Scores. Fair Isaac credit reporting agency scores are used by lenders and others to assess the credit risk of prospective borrowers or existing customers, in order to help make credit and marketing decisions." These scores are derived solely from the information available on credit reporting agency reports. Credit Score is a term often used to refer to credit reporting agency risk scores. It broadly refers to a number generated by a statistical model which is used to objectively evaluate information that pertains to making a credit decision. For a fee, you can obtain your FICO Score online at www.myfico.com.

report and score at the same time. For this, you'll be charged approximately $6 per score.

You can also contact each of the three credit reporting agencies separately (see the contact information in the previous section) to purchase your credit score in conjunction with a credit report or separately. For example, from Experian, you can purchase a single credit report with corresponding credit score for $15, or just obtain your credit score for $5.95.

The Benefits of a Three-in-One Credit Report and How to Obtain One

Many companies, including the three major credit reporting companies, offer comprehensive, three-in-one credit reports. On one single report, you receive detailed information from all three credit agencies. This allows you to quickly review and compare content from all three reports at once, and saves you from having to flip between the three separate reports as you analyze your current situation. The price you pay for a three-in-one report will vary, based on the company you use to retrieve it and whether the corresponding credit scores are included.

TIP

It's definitely a good idea to purchase your credit score at the same time you obtain a copy of your credit report. Simply by reviewing your credit report, it's virtually impossible for a consumer to manually calculate or even estimate what their corresponding credit score is, yet this is a vital piece of information that will ultimately determine whether or not you're credit worthy or approved for a loan.

For someone who is extremely interested in tracking their credit report and credit score on an ongoing basis, subscribing to a credit monitoring service is a worthwhile investment. For example, TransUnion offers unlimited access to your constantly updated three-in-one credit report (with corresponding credit scores), and notifies you anytime a change is made to your credit report. The fee for this credit monitoring service is $24.95 for the first month, then $14.95 per month thereafter.

Without subscribing to a credit monitoring service, expect to pay between $30 and $40 for a single three-in-one credit report, plus a bit extra if you want your credit scores. In addition to Equifax, Experian, and TransUnion, many other companies also offer the ability to order a three-in-one credit report online.

☆ ☆ **WARNING** ☆ ☆

Before ordering a credit report, a three-in-one credit report or credit monitoring service from a company that isn't one of the three major credit reporting agencies (credit bureaus), make sure the company is legitimate. You will need to provide personal information, including your name, date of birth, address, and Social Security number, which is data that could easily be used for identity theft or other fraudulent purposes.

TIP

When shopping for a credit monitoring service, ideally you want to receive unlimited access to your three-in-one credit report, with accompanying credit scores, for the lowest monthly fee possible. Some services offer one month free, then begin charging. Others charge extra to obtain your credit scores. Before signing up for a service, make sure you understand what's included, plus what the monthly fee is. Also, determine if there's a one-time start-up fee or if there's a cancellation fee.

The data provided on a three-in-one credit report will be identical to the data you'd receive by requesting separate credit reports from all three credit reporting agencies. The difference is in how the data is formatted.

You Have Your Credit Report, Now What?

The process for obtaining your credit report may sound a bit confusing, but the process is relatively quick and simple, especially if you're obtaining free reports from the Annual Credit Report Request Service or purchasing reports from one of the three major credit reporting agencies.

After obtaining your reports, the next step is to review the information included within each of them. Make sure all of the information is up-to-date and accurate. If you notice errors in any of the three reports, it's important to take the necessary steps to correct the error(s) as quickly as possible. If the error involves information provided by a creditor, begin by contacting the creditor directly. The creditor's name and contact information should be listed on your credit report. If you're unable to correct the error or initiate a dispute directly with the creditor, contact the credit reporting agency that provided the report with the incorrect information. The process for correcting inaccuracies in your credit report is described within Chapter 4.

Dispute. If you find an error in the information listed on your credit report, you have a right to initiate a dispute with the creditor and/or credit reporting agency. By law, a dispute must be investigated within 30 days. If the information is, in fact, inaccurate, it must then be corrected, causing your credit report and potentially your credit score to be revised.

TIP

If you notice errors in the personal information section of your credit report, such as the spelling of your name, your date of birth, or address, contact the appropriate credit reporting agency directly to correct these errors.

Errors in your credit report can be disputed online, by calling the credit reporting agencies, or in writing. For the quickest response, dispute errors online. Visit each credit reporting agency's web site and follow the appropriate links.

- *Equifax*, www.equifax.com. From the web site's home page, click on the "Online Dispute" icon located at the top of the page, then follow the directions provided. You can also call (800) 493-1058 during business hours.
- *Experian*, www.experian.com. From the web site's home page, click on the "Submit A Dispute Online" icon to begin the process. You can also call (800) 493-1058 during business hours.
- *TransUnion*, www.transunion.com. From the web site's home page, click on the "Personal Solutions" icon. Next, on the left side of the page, click on the "Dispute Credit Report" icon. You can also call (800) 916-8800 during business hours.

What Your Creditors Have to Say on Your Credit Report

As you learned in Chapter 1, credit reports are divided into several sections, designed to make the reports easier to read and understand. The order in which these sections appear and their formats will vary, depending on the credit reporting agency and how the credit report was obtained.

TIP

To view a sample credit report from Experian, point your web browser to: www.experian.com/credit_report_basics/pdf/samplecreditreport1.pdf.

All credit reports for consumers begin with a "Report Summary." This includes your name, the Report Number, and the date the report was issued. You'll also find a short summary of the potentially negative and positive pieces of information found within the report. If you need to contact any of the credit reporting agencies in reference to information on your report, to initiate a dispute, for example, you will need to provide the Report Number included on your credit report.

Each item listed on your credit report is called a *Trade Line*—whether it's a mortgage, car loan, student loan, credit card, charge card, or other type of loan. For each Trade Line, you will see detailed information on your credit report, which includes:

- *The creditor's name.* This will be the name of the creditor or collection agency that has reported the information to the credit reporting agency.
- *The creditor's address.* This is the mailing address of the creditor.
- *The creditor's phone number.* This is the phone number you should use to contact the creditor to make a payment,

make a settlement offer, to initiate a dispute or to get a question answered. If no phone number is listed for the creditor, contact the credit reporting agency directly or call directory assistance.

- *Account number*. This is your account number associated with your account or loan. Displayed here might be your loan number, credit card number, or other customer identification number. For security purposes, some creditors list only the first or last few digits of an account number.

- *Status/remark*. This describes the current status of the account. It might read, "Open/Current," "Paid As Agreed," "Collection Account," "Paid, Closed/Never Late," "Account closed at consumer's request," "Paid in settlement," "Placed for collection," "Closed," or some variation that describes whether or not the account is active and in good standing. When you see "Open/Current" displayed as the status of an item listed in your credit report, it means the account is open, active, paid up-to-date, and is in good standing. This is the ideal status you want for each current listing on your credit reports.

- *Date opened*. This is the date the account was first opened.

- *Type*. Here, the type of account is listed. On your credit report, it might read, "Revolving," "Credit Card," "Collection," "Automobile," "Mortgage," or "Installment," for example. A "Revolving" account typically refers to a credit card.

- *Credit limit/original amount.* The amount of the original loan will be listed here, if the item is for some type of loan (such as a mortgage or car loan). The credit limit will be listed here if the accounts related to a credit or charge card.

- *Reported since.* This is the date that the credit reporting agency first started receiving information about the account.

- *Terms.* Details about the loan, if applicable, will be displayed here. For example, for a mortgage, the monthly payment and length of the mortgage will be listed. In many situations, the 'Terms' section may be blank or contain the letters "NA," meaning "Not Applicable."

- *High balance.* This is the highest balance the consumer has put on the account. If it's a mortgage or car loan, for example, the original loan amount will be listed. For charge cards, the highest balance put on the card to date will be listed.

- *Date of status.* This is the date on which the Status section was last updated.

- *Monthly payment.* Depending on the type of account, the monthly payment the consumer is responsible for will be listed here.

- *Recent balance.* Here you'll find the most recent balance owed on the account.

- *Last reported.* This is the date the creditor last reported information about the account to the credit reporting agency.
- *Responsibility.* This states whether it's an individual or joint account and who is responsible for it.
- *Recent payment.* The amount of the last payment received is displayed.
- *Account history.* This section summarizes the account status on a month-by-month basis, typically over a several year period, if applicable.

Figuring Out What Needs to Happen Next

The reason you requested a copy of your credit report will ultimately determine what happens next. If you notice any inaccuracies, see Chapter 4. If you believe you're a victim of identity theft because you discover items on your credit report that don't belong to you, such as credit cards in your name that you never applied for and never received, it's important to take action quickly. See the "Identity Theft Emergencies" section later in this chapter.

If you're like a huge percentage of the U.S. population, chances are you'll find some negative information listed on your credit reports. Determine if this negative information can be corrected or improved upon by contacting the creditor, paying an outstanding debt, or changing your spending habits so you'll be able to pay your bills on time in the future.

> **TIP**
>
> On the day you review your credit report, make a note in your daily planner to review an updated credit report in six to 12 months. This is something you should get in the habit of doing, especially if you don't subscribe to a credit monitoring service.

Chapter 5 offers easy strategies you can begin implementing immediately to improve your credit score.

If you plan to apply for a mortgage, hope to refinance your mortgage, apply for some other type of loan, or plan to apply for new credit cards, based on the information you discover on your credit report and by evaluating your credit score, you'll be in a better position to determine whether you'll qualify (and at what interest rates) based on your credit worthiness. This will allow you to take the appropriate steps to move your plans forward. Chapter 6 will help you proceed.

Identity Theft Emergencies

Discovering you've become a victim of identity theft or some other type of credit fraud can be an extremely stressful and costly experience if not handled swiftly and correctly. Out of the over $1 trillion in current credit card consumer debt (as of early 2006), it's estimated that credit card fraud represents $2 to $3 billion. Although you may be protected financially if you're a fraud victim, correcting the problem will still often require a significant time commitment on your part.

 Identity Theft. This is the unauthorized use of personal identification information to commit fraud or other crimes. This could include someone using your credit card(s) to make unauthorized purchases or use your identity to take out loans or establish credit in your name.

Before you think to yourself, "Oh, that could never happen to me," consider these disturbing statistics offered by the Federal Trade Commission:

- In 2003, there were over 9,910,000 victims of identity theft.
- In 2004, identity theft resulted in $47,600,000,000 in losses within the United States alone.

TIP

The best way to prevent identity theft is to subscribe to a credit monitoring service so you will be notified within 24 hours every time any type of change is made to your credit report. Thus, if someone uses your identity to apply for a credit card or some type of loan, for example, you will find out about it immediately and can stop it before it's too late.

- For victims of identity theft, it will require a time investment of 175 to 600 hours (or more) to recover their good names and recover from the identity theft.
- There's a new identity theft victim in the United States every four seconds.

How can you determine if you're a victim of identity theft? There are several warning signs to be on the lookout for, including:

- Your credit reports will list new credit cards as having been issued in your name that you never applied for or received.
- Your credit reports will list information about accounts that you did not open and know nothing about.
- You'll notice charges on your monthly credit card statements and/or bank statements that you didn't authorize.
- You stop receiving monthly credit card statements or important bills altogether.
- You begin receiving bills from companies you've never done business with.
- You begin receiving calls from creditors and/or collection agencies about accounts you know nothing about.

If you believe you've become a victim of identity theft or some type of credit-related fraud, here are some steps to follow:

- Contact your creditors and bank immediately to discuss your suspicions. If you've had a credit card lost or stolen (or you notice potentially fraudulent charges on your statement), report that immediately to the bank or credit card issuer. The appropriate phone number will be listed on your statement and on your credit card.

- Contact your local police department immediately and file a report. Be sure to obtain a copy of this report.

- Collect all documents, such as your credit report, monthly statements, or other written information that relate to your suspicion. Begin keeping detailed notes about with whom you speak and what notices you receive. Do not destroy or throw away any related paperwork or files.

- If you believe someone is fraudulently using your Social Security number, contact the Social Security Administration.

- Change your password and PIN on all ATM, debit, and credit cards. Have your checking account number (and related passwords and PINs) changed as well.

- Contact the Fraud Victim Assistance department at each of the major credit reporting agencies. Ask that a "Fraud Alert" be placed in your credit report file. From this point forward, creditors will be instructed to take additional steps to verify your identity before granting you (or someone impersonating you) credit. Contact: Equifax (800-525-6285), Experian (888-397-3742), and TransUnion (800-860-7289). Remember, contacting just one of the credit reporting agencies isn't sufficient. All three must be contacted.

TIP

The Federal Trade Commission can also be helpful if you're a victim of identity theft. Contact the Identity Theft Data Clearing House at (877) ID-THEFT or visit www.consumer.gov/ idtheft. Once you report your identity theft or fraud suspicions, you may be required to complete an ID Theft Affidavit and/or a Fraudulent Account Statement. A group of credit grantors, consumer advocates, and the FTC developed these forms to help consumers report information to many companies using one standard form. This form can be obtained by calling the FTC's Identity Theft Data Clearing House or visiting the organization's web site.

Misconceptions and Bad Information Can Lead to Costly Mistakes

For a variety of reasons, personal finances and credit can be extremely confusing topics. People have many misconceptions people have about credit that can ultimately lead to costly mistakes or problems.

Having the right information and acting appropriately based on the information you know is correct and using your own common sense will help you boost your credit score, better manage your personal finances, avoid becoming a victim of identity theft and ultimately save you a fortune. Now that you have a current copy of your credit report(s) in-hand, you're in a much better position to analyze your personal situation, and if necessary, take steps to improve upon it.

CHAPTER 4

How to Update or Fix
Your Credit Report

WHAT'S IN THIS CHAPTER

- ➤ Determining what information can legitimately be edited or removed from your credit reports.

- ➤ How to correct errors on your credit reports and initiate a dispute.

- ➤ How to get other information edited or changed on your credit reports, even if the information is negative, but accurately being reported.

Reviewing Your Credit Reports

By following the advice in Chapter 3, you should have no trouble acquiring copies of your credit reports from Experian, Equifax, and TransUnion by phone, mail, or within minutes online. With copies of each credit report in hand, or after purchasing a three-in-one credit report, you'll need to spend time evaluating each trade line of each report.

During your evaluation, examine each trade line carefully. Determine if the information being reported on each credit report is positive, negative, or inaccurate. If the information is positive, chances are it's helping to boost your credit score and it's based on the fact that you're up-to-date and in good standing with that creditor or lender. This will be reflected in the "Status" section of each trade line, which ideally should read "Paid As Agreed" or "Open/Current."

☆ ☆ **WARNING** ☆ ☆

If you discover a trade line on your credit report that lists an account that does not belong to you, you could be a victim of identity theft. See Chapter 3 for details on how to deal with this situation.

If any information in your credit reports is negative, it could be there because of late or missed payments or as a result of somehow mismanaging your credit. In this situation, you need to identify what the cause of the problem is and figure out the best way to rectify it. This might mean changing your habits and paying your bills on time in the future. It might mean making an effort to lower your outstanding balances. If the debt is long overdue or has gone to collections, remedying the situation may require you to contact the creditor or lender directly and negotiate in order to achieve a favorable solution. As you already know, having negative information that's accurately being reported to the credit reporting agencies and that appears on your credit report is difficult to remove within a seven-year period, unless you negotiate directly with the creditor or lender.

Upon reviewing your credit reports and perhaps comparing the information to your current statements, you may discover some errors. If these errors are in the Personal Information section of your credit report where your name, address, telephone number(s), Social Security number, date of birth, and employment information is listed, directly contact the credit reporting agency whoo provided you with the credit report containing the error. Errors in the Personal Information section of your credit report do not impact your credit score, but they should still be corrected. You'll discover how to do this later in the chapter.

In the "Potentially Negative Items" section of your credit report, you'll find trade lines that contain some type of negative data that is hurting your credit score. The items listed in this section are the ones that potential creditors and lenders will look at carefully before making their decisions. From this information, a potential creditor or lender can easily determine the cause of the negative information, such as late payments, determine how late the payments are or have been, and discover how much money is currently owed or past due.

As you review the information in this section, make sure it's accurate and up-to-date. Keep in mind, a payment you made to the creditor or lender less than 30 days earlier might not yet have registered on your credit report. Only if you discover inaccurate information should you initiate a *dispute* with the credit reporting agency that supplied the credit report.

Dispute. If you notice an error in your credit report, the process of having it investigated and hopefully corrected by the credit reporting agencies is done by initiating a dispute. Once a dispute is filed (either by phone, mail, or online), the credit reporting agency will immediately contact the creditor or lender and begin an investigation. The outcome of the investigation will be reflected on your credit report within 30 days. If the error you disputed is, in fact, an error, it will be corrected and

TIP

In some cases, you may need to dispute the same inaccurate item on two or all three of your credit reports, depending on the information the lender or creditor has supplied to the credit reporting agencies.

> **TIP**
>
> Initiating a dispute costs nothing and can be done online quickly. However, a dispute can also be initiated by telephone or by sending a letter in the mail to the appropriate credit reporting agency.

your credit report will be updated accordingly. Negative information that is being accurately reported, however, cannot be removed from your credit report by initiating a dispute.

After reviewing the "Potentially Negative" items section of your credit report, continue to carefully review the remainder of each report, including the "Credit Items" section which lists all of the trade lines being reported to the credit collection agency, as well as the "Accounts in Good Standing" section which displays the information on your report that's favorable.

On a separate sheet of paper, as you're reviewing your credit reports, make a note of trade lines that contain negative information that you need to be addressed, plus a list of inaccuracies on each report that need to be corrected.

What Information Can Be Edited or Removed from Your Credit Reports

Remember, only information that is inaccurate can be disputed and ultimately removed easily by initiating a dispute

TIP

If you have a legitimate reason for negative information appearing on your credit report, you have the right to add a "Personal Statement" to each of your credit reports. This is a short, text item you can add by contacting the credit reporting agencies. This statement will have no impact on your credit score, but it will be read by anyone who manually reviews your credit report. A Personal Statement must be under 100 words in length. Make sure you have the Personal Statement removed after the situation described in your statement has been corrected or resolved. Otherwise, it could remain on your credit report indefinitely. If you've had a medical emergency, illness, or lost your job, this can be explained in your Personal Statement.

directly with the credit reporting agencies. If you want negative but accurate information removed from your credit report(s), you'll need to negotiate with each creditor separately.

How to Correct Errors

There are two basic ways to correct errors on your credit report:

1. Contact the creditor or lender directly via telephone or mail.

2. Initiate a dispute with the appropriate credit reporting agencies, based on which of your credit reports include the erroneous data.

If, however, you're trying to "fix" negative information that's accurately being reported to the credit bureaus, you'll need to negotiate with your creditors directly. The credit reporting agencies will only remove data from a credit report that's proven to be false.

Contacting and Negotiating with Your Creditors

The process of creditors and lenders reporting information on an ongoing monthly basis to the credit reporting agencies is purely voluntary. *Any information that a creditor adds to your credit report could theoretically be removed, if you can convince the creditor to take this action.*

If you're dealing with a collection agency working on behalf of a creditor, that agency's job is to collect the debt. Negotiating will be more difficult, but certainly isn't impossible, especially if the account is seriously past due and you're interested in negotiating a full payoff, settlement, or payment plan.

Depending on your financial and credit situation, in terms of fixing negative information that's listed on your credit report without further hurting your credit score in the future, consider trying to renegotiate your payment schedule with the creditor. They may be willing to lower your monthly payments, defer one or more payments, waive late fees, and

---

TIP

A collection agency that is working on behalf of a creditor is different from a collection agency that has purchased your debt outright from the original creditor or lender. If a collection agency or law firm has purchased the debt, which is something that would happen after it has been charged off or written off by the original creditor or lender, you must now deal directly with that collection agency or law firm that now has full authority in regard to that debt.

---

penalties, lower your interest rate, or somehow restructure the loan to make paying it off more achievable based on your current situation.

An alternative to restructuring the payment schedule is to offer a settlement to the creditor. This is a legally binding agreement that allows you to renegotiate the amount owed. In many cases, this will stop interest, late fees, and other charges from accruing as you pay off the amount due, which can often be reduced. The problem with negotiating a settlement and paying off less than the amount originally owed is that settlements are typically listed on your credit report for seven years and detract from your credit score for that entire time, even after the account is paid off and closed.

Settlements need to be negotiated with the creditor. You need to negotiate how much is owed, how the repayment plan

---

will be structured and what the outcome on your credit report will be once the debt is paid off. All settlements should ultimately be put in writing by the creditor or lender.

☆ ☆ **WARNING** ☆ ☆

If you set up a payment plan as part of your settlement, failure to meet your obligations on time could cause the original terms of the debt to be reinstated. This means interest, penalties, late fees, and legal fees could all be added to the amount due. It also increases the chances that the creditor or collection agency will take you to court or take whatever legal action they can to collect the debt.

When negotiating with a creditor, your ultimate objective is to convince them to list the account as "Paid as Agreed," "Current," or "Account Closed—Paid as Agreed" with each of the credit bureaus. Anything other than that will negatively impact your credit score. Your willingness to negotiate and a demonstration of good faith with proper follow through on your promises will help you achieve this objective.

If during the negotiation you're told the person your dealing with who works for the creditor or lender doesn't have the authority to change how the account is being reported to the credit reporting agencies, insist on speaking with someone who does have that authority, such as a supervisor. Whether you pay an account that's gone to collections is irrelevant to your credit score unless the account is reported to the credit collection agencies as "Paid as Agreed" or "Account Closed—Paid as Agreed."

Listings on your credit report to avoid include: "Paid," "Paid—Charge Off," "Settled," "Repossession," and "Paid—[insert number of days] Days Late." Any of these will have a negative impact on your credit score for up to seven years and impact your ability to obtain credit in the future, even if the overdue amount is ultimately paid in full or you pay the amount agreed to as part of a settlement.

Many creditors will agree to alter how your account is being reported to the credit reporting agencies if the settlement involves you paying at least 70 percent of the amount due, and you meet the obligations of the settlement with no further delays. As you're negotiating, you'll have more leverage in terms of reducing your settlement amount if you can make one lump sum payment as opposed to setting up a payment plan

---

TIP

When dealing with collection agencies especially, you should pay off your debts or make settlement payments using a money order or cashier's check. If you pay using a personal check, you'll be providing that agency with your checking account information, which may not be in your best interest.

---

over a period of months or years. The decision to negotiate with a consumer and ultimately change how information is reported to the credit reporting agencies is made on a case-by-case basis and will depend on your ability to negotiate with the creditor or lender. It is not normal policy to delete negative information from a consumer's credit report just because the debt is paid after it has been late or has gone to collections.

☆ ☆ **WARNING** ☆ ☆

When sending a letter to your creditor(s), be sure to use the correct address. The address you typically send payments to is almost always different from the creditor's business office. In most cases, you can use the contact information for the creditor or collection agency that's listed on your credit report.

☆ ☆ **WARNING** ☆ ☆

Anything you say could be held against you! When speaking or corresponding with a debt collector, creditor, or collection agency, your phone calls are typically recorded and anything you say could potentially be used in court. Always act professionally and refrain from lying or making threats.

Quick Tips to Help Your Negotiations

When you're negotiating with creditors, their job is to collect the money you owe using tactics that are within the boundaries of the law. They may be overly pushy, obnoxious, or rude. After all, they're accustomed to dealing with deadbeats who don't pay their bills. It's your job to protect your own interests, while at the same time, living up to your financial and legal obligations. Someone who works for a collection agency, for example, does *not* have your best interests in mind, despite whatever they say. They don't care about your problems. They just want to collect the money that's due to them or the company they represent.

Here are some tips to help you negotiate with a creditor or collection agency:

- If you make a request that is denied for whatever reason, ask to speak with a supervisor.
- Don't agree to pay more than you can afford when negotiating. Know in advance what your financial situation really is, then work within those confines. The last thing you want to do is negotiate a settlement or payment plan that you can't afford to adhere to.
- During your negotiating process, figure out what the creditor is willing to accept as a settlement. What's their absolute bottom line? If you're looking for a settlement, offering between 50 and 70 percent of what's owed, either as a lump sum payment or through a payment plan isn't unreasonable.

- Try to avoid becoming intimidated by the person you're negotiating with, even if they make threats about lawsuits.

- Keep in mind, most successful negotiations require several rounds going back and forth with offers and counter offers. The process could take days or weeks.

- If you can afford to settle an account by paying one lump sum (as opposed to using a payment plan), you'll have more negotiating leverage.

- The person you're negotiating with does this for a living and is a trained professional when it comes to debt collections. For them to use legal terminology during a conversation or in writing is a common tactic to confuse or intimidate you. Listen carefully to what's being said and make sure you understand exactly what you're committing to. Consult with a lawyer or credit counselor if you have questions.

- Make sure everything you ultimately agree to is put in writing, signed, and dated by both parties.

As part of your negotiation, some of the things you could potentially ask for include:

- A lower interest rate
- For the interest accrued to be waived
- For the late fees, penalties, and/or legal fees to be waived
- For the loan to be extended or restructured, allowing you to skip one or more payments with no penalty

- A payment plan that would allow you to pay off the amount currently owed, but with no added interest or fees added in the future
- A settlement that would include a significantly lower balance due (such as 50 to 75 percent of the total)
- Favorable reporting to the credit reporting agencies or the removal of negative information from your credit report

If you're being harassed by creditors or collection agencies (or law firms representing them), you have some legal rights even if you owe the money. Be sure to review the Federal Fair Debt Collection Practices Act so you know what your rights are. Collection agents cannot abuse, threaten or harass you, provide you with false or misleading information, or use unfair practices to collect the monies due.

To read the Federal Fair Debt Collection Practices Act, point your web browser to: www.ftc.gov/os/statutes/fdcpa/ fdcpact.htm. You can also learn more about debt collection practices by visiting the FTC's web site at www.ftc.gov/bcp/ conline/pubs/credit/fdc.htm. An easier-to-read, two-page summary of the Federal Fair Debt Collection Practices Act, which outlines your rights as a consumer, can be found at: www.ftc.gov/bcp/conline/pubs/credit/fcrasummary.pdf.

According to the FTC, "A debt collector is any person who regularly collects debts owed to others. This includes attorneys who collect debts on a regular basis. A collector may contact you in person, by mail, telephone or fax. However, a debt collector may not contact you at inconvenient times or places, such as before 8 A.M. or after 9 P.M., unless you agree. A debt collector also may not contact you at work if the collector knows that your employer disapproves of such contacts."

Furthermore, according to the FTC, "You can stop a debt collector from contacting you by writing a letter to the collector telling them to stop. Once the collector receives your letter, they may not contact you again except to say there will be no further contact or to notify you that the debt collector or the creditor intends to take some specific action." Sending such a letter to a collector does *not* make the debt magically disappear if you actually owe it. You could still be sued by the debt collector or your original creditor, which is a greater possibility if you demonstrate no interest in paying off or otherwise settling the debt.

"If you have an attorney, the debt collector must contact the attorney, rather than you. If you do not have an attorney, a collector may contact other people, but only to find out where you live, what your phone number is, and where you work. Collectors usually are prohibited from contacting such third parties more than once. In most cases, the collector may not tell anyone other than you and your attorney that you owe money. Within five days after you are first contacted, the collector must send you a written notice telling you the amount of money you owe; the name of the creditor to whom you owe the money; and what action to take if you believe you do not owe the money," reports the FTC.

By law, a debt collector may not harass, oppress, or abuse you. Thus, the use threats of violence or harm; publishing a list of consumers who refuse to pay their debts (except to a credit reporting agency); use obscene or profane language; or repeatedly use the telephone to annoy someone is forbidden. It's also illegal for a debt collector to make false or misleading statements when attempting to collect a debt.

For example, the debt collector cannot falsely imply that he or she is an attorney or a government representative; imply that you have committed a crime; falsely represent that they operate or work for a credit reporting agency; misrepresent the amount of your debt; imply that papers that were sent to you are legal forms when they were not; or misrepresent that papers being sent to you are not legal forms when they are. These are all guidelines issued by the FTC that debt collectors must adhere to.

☆ ☆ **WARNING** ☆ ☆

All debt collectors know the law and are extremely familiar with the Fair Debt Collection Act. However, some less reputable debt collectors will find ways to push the limits of the law in order to achieve their objectives. If you believe a debt collector has violated the law in its dealings with you, consider hiring an attorney or contact the Federal Trade Commission at (877) 382-4357.

The FTC reports that some of the others things a debt collector may not do in an effort to collect money owed include:

- Giving false credit information about you to anyone, including a credit collection agency.
- Sending you anything that looks like an official document from a court or government agency when it is not.
- Contacting you via postcard (as opposed to a letter in a sealed envelope).
- Using a false name when contacting you.
- Collecting an amount greater than your debt, unless your state law permits such a charge. The additional charges could include legal fees incurred by the original lender, creditor, or debt collector.
- Depositing a post-dated check prematurely.
- Using deception to trick you into accepting costly collect calls.
- Taking or threatening to take your property unless this can be done legally.

Communicating with Your Creditors in Writing

Any correspondence between you and your creditors or debt collectors, especially settlement or pay-off offers and agreements, should always be put in writing. Be sure to keep copies of all correspondence. When sending your correspondence, use a method that will show proof of receipt. From the U.S. Post Office, you can send a letter and add Delivery Confirmation, for example. In your letters, be sure your full name, address, phone number, and account number are listed. If you send a fax, follow it up by sending a hard copy of the fax via the mail or overnight courier.

Initiating Disputes with the Credit Reporting Agencies

Thanks to computers, initiating disputes with the credit reporting agencies is a relatively easy process. If the dispute is initiated online, you can typically have the issue resolved within about 10 days, although legally the credit reporting agencies have up to 30 days to investigate your dispute.

Before a dispute is made, you must obtain a copy of your credit report from each credit reporting agency you'll be filing a dispute with. You will need the credit report number that's listed on the first page of each credit report.

Filing a dispute will force the credit reporting agency to initiate an investigation, during which time the creditor or lender will be contacted and asked to provide proof that the information being reported is, in fact, accurate. If no proof is

---

TIP

If you discover the same error on all three of your credit reports, you will need to initiate a dispute for that item separately with all three credit reporting agencies or contact the creditor directly.

TIP

Initiating disputes with the credit reporting agencies online will save you a lot of time. If the dispute is initiated via the mail, it will take longer for the investigation to get underway and be completed.

provided and the information on the credit report is really erroneous, it must be corrected within 30 days.

Follow these steps for initiating a dispute online:

1. Obtain a copy of your credit report from each credit reporting agency.
2. Make a note of the credit report number listed on the top of each report. If the credit report you received doesn't have a credit report number, you will need to obtain a new copy of your credit report directly from that credit reporting agency or from the Annual Credit Report (www.AnnualCreditReport.com) web site. Upon obtaining a credit report, the credit report number you receive will remain active for a period of 90 days.
3. Review each credit report carefully and identify errors you wish to dispute.
4. Point your web browser to the appropriate credit reporting agency's web site.
   - Experian, www.experian.com/disputes/index.html
   - Equifax, www.equifax.com/dispute

- TransUnion, www.transunion.com. Click on the "Personal Solutions" icon followed by the "Dispute Credit Report" icon.

5. Click on the appropriate icon on the credit reporting agency's web site to initiate an online dispute.

6. You'll be asked to enter your credit report number, plus additional information about yourself to verify your identity. This information may include your Social Security number, date of birth, the state where you live, and/or your zip code.

7. You will be asked to approve a Terms and Conditions statement from the credit reporting agency that appears on your computer screen.

8. Once you're looking at your credit report on the computer screen, click on the particular item(s) that you believe are inaccurate, then click on the "Dispute Item" icon that's displayed.

9. You'll need to select a specific reason for the dispute and choose one of the options that explains why you believe the information is incorrect. Depending on the type of listing, options will include: "Payment never late," "No knowledge of account," "Account paid in full," "Account closed," "Unauthorized Charges," "Belonged to ex-spouse," "Balance incorrect," "Included in bankruptcy," "Belongs to primary account holder," "Corporate account," "Balance history inaccurate," or "Other reason." You can also add your

own brief statement (up to 120 characters) explaining why the information is inaccurate.

10. You will be asked to provide your e-mail address so you can be contacted with the results of the investigation.

11. Upon completing this online dispute process, an investigation will immediately begin. You will be notified of the outcome within 30 days (unusually within 10 days).

12. If your investigation concludes and the result is not in your favor, but you have evidence or information to substantiate your claim, initiate another dispute in writing and include copies of your information and evidence or contact the creditor directly.

To initiate a dispute in writing, you will first need to obtain a copy of your credit report containing a current credit report number. Next, determine what information is inaccurate. This information will need to be put in writing in the form of a letter addressed to the appropriate credit collection agency.

The letter should contain the following information:

- Your full name, address, and phone number
- Your date of birth
- Your Social Security number
- The credit report number
- A photocopy of your picture ID (such as a driver's license or passport), plus a copy of a recent utility bill that displays your name and address.

- A separate listing for each error and why you believe the information is incorrect. It's helpful to include a photocopy of your credit report or the trade lines that you're disputing.

Mail your letter, along with any additional information or evidence, to the appropriate credit reporting agency using the following addresses. You can also call each credit reporting agency to initiate a dispute using the following phone numbers:

Experian
P.O. Box 2002
Allen, TX 75013
(888) 397-3742 or (800) 493-1058

Equifax Credit Information Services, Inc.
P.O. Box 740241
Atlanta, GA 30374
(800) 685-1111

TransUnion
P.O. Box 2000
Chester, PA 19022-2000
(800) 916-8800

Working with a Credit Counseling Company

Depending on your personal situation, you can initiate disputes and negotiate with creditors on your own behalf, or you could hire a professional credit counselor. For more information on credit counseling services, see Chapter 7.

What to Do Next

Once you've initiated a dispute with either a creditor or the credit reporting agencies, stay on top of the situation. If you don't receive a response within 30 days, initiate contact again or contact the credit reporting agencies directly. Unfortunately, not all negative information can or will voluntarily be removed by your creditors, even if you pay off or settle your accounts. To have the negative information removed, you will need to negotiate with the creditor and make the change to your credit report regarding a condition of the pay-off or settlement.

When negative information exists on your credit report, it will lower your credit score. It then becomes even more necessary to take steps to improve your credit score and rebuild your credit. This is a process that will take a multifaceted approach over the next six to 12 months, or perhaps several years, depending on your financial situation. In Chapter 5, you'll discover multiple strategies you can begin implementing to improve your credit score and reduce the impact negative information on your credit report has on your credit score.

CHAPTER 5

Ten Strategies to Improve Your Credit **Report and Boost Your Credit Score**

WHAT'S IN THIS CHAPTER

➢ Strategies you can begin implementing immediately to start cleaning up your own credit report and improving your credit score.

➢ Avoiding popular credit repair scams.

Having a Poor Credit Score Will Cost You Big Bucks

The information on your credit report directly impacts your credit score. In fact, it's the only thing that impacts your score. Your credit score in turn determines your ability to obtain credit and potentially be approved for loans. Having a poor credit score will either keep you from obtaining credit altogether or place you in a high-risk category, which means that if you are approved for credit or loans, the interest rates you'll be offered will be significantly higher than someone with excellent credit. Over the life of a mortgage, home equity loan, car loan, or student loan, for example, this can cost you tens of thousands of dollars in interest fees.

For example, if you apply for a $250,000, 30-year, fixed-rate mortgage and your credit score is between 760 and 800 (which is excellent), you could qualify for a rate of 5.9 percent. This would make your monthly payment $1482.84. Someone with a credit score of between 660 and 679 might qualify for an interest rate of 6.51 percent for that same loan. Thus, their monthly payment would be $1581.81. Someone with a credit score of 620 to 639 might qualify for an interest rate of 7.49 percent. This would make their monthly payment $1746.32.

In this example, the person with the credit score between 600 and 679 would pay $1,187.84 per year extra in interest compared to the person with the excellent credit score of between 760 and 800. Over the 30-year term of the loan, that's an extra $35,629.20 in interest fees alone. Meanwhile, the person with the credit score between 620 and 639 would pay $3,161.76 per year extra in interest compared to the person with excellent credit score of 760 and 800. This means that over the term of the loan, the person with the lower credit score would pay $94,852.80 extra in interest compared to someone with what would be considered excellent credit.

Your Actions Impact Your Credit Worthiness

If you currently have an above average or excellent credit score, it's important to maintain it. Far too many people do stupid things, like making mortgage payments late or skipping credit card payments, and the negative impact on their credit scores is disastrous. Just one late mortgage payment that gets listed on your credit report could cause you to be rejected or be offered a significantly higher interest rate (with extra fees attached to the loan) if you attempt to refinance your mortgage, need to apply for a new mortgage as a result of a move, or apply for a home equity (or home improvement) loan or second mortgage.

If your credit score is already below average as a result of poor decisions and irresponsible financial actions in your past, it's important to immediately begin rectifying the situation by taking steps to begin rebuilding your credit. This process can take months or even years of diligence and responsible financial planning.

This chapter focuses on ten strategies and tips for improving the information on your credit report, which will lead to a boost in your credit score. Unfortunately, successfully completing just one or two of these tasks probably won't result in a fast and dramatic jump in your credit score. However, utilizing most or all of these strategies simultaneously over time will definitely give your credit score upward momentum, the results of which you should start seeing within 6 to 12 months (possibly sooner), depending on your unique situation.

When it comes to repairing or rebuilding your credit, this is definitely something you can do yourself. There are, however, legitimate credit counselors, financial planners, and accountants who can assist you in better managing your finances and in learning to be more responsible when it comes to managing your credit.

Strategy 1. Pay Your Bills on Time

This strategy may seem extremely obvious, however, late payments are the most common piece of negative information that appears on peoples' credit reports and is often responsible for significant drops in credit scores. When it comes to loans and credit cards, it's vital that you always make at least the minimum payments in a timely manner each and every month, with no exceptions.

The impact on your credit report and credit score will be considerable if you're late or skip one or more mortgage payments, however, making late payments on other types of loans or defaulting on any loans will also have a disastrous impact on your credit score that will have an impact for up to seven years.

> **TIP**
>
> As you discovered in Chapter 2, your credit score is calcu-
> lated based on a complex formula that is directly impacted
> by your payment history, the amounts owed, the length of your cred-
> it history, new credit, the types of credit you've utilized, and the num-
> ber of credit inquiries you've had. Your payment history is weighted
> the heaviest in this calculation, with late payments, collection
> accounts, defaulted loans, repossessions, and other negative pay-
> ment history information all working against you and causing your
> credit score to drop.

The benefit to having credit cards is that you can determine how much you spend using them, then decide how
much you wish to pay back each month, as long as that
amount is equal to or greater than the minimum monthly payment due. This allows you to budget your money and make
intelligent decisions, based on your financial situation. Simply
paying the minimums on your credit cards will keep those
accounts from being late, however, the costs associated with
that decision (in terms of fees and interest) will often be significant over time. Plus, this strategy will keep you from greatly
reducing or paying off the debt.

One of the worst mistakes you can make, aside from
making late mortgage payments, is having an account go to

collections. This means that you've neglected to pay your monthly minimums or have skipped payments for several months and the account gets turned over to a collection agency. Once this happens, regardless of whether or not you ultimately make the payments or settle the account, your credit score will be negatively impacted for up to seven years.

☆ ☆ **WARNING** ☆ ☆

It's important to understand that decisions you make now, and the actions you take in terms of paying or not paying your creditors in a timely manner can impact your credit report for many years to come. A negative piece of information placed on your credit report this month will cause your credit score to drop. However, the impact of the information on your credit report (and its impact on your credit score) could haunt you for seven years (or longer). A few bad decisions today could keep you from buying or leasing a new car, getting approved for a mortgage, or qualifying for credit cards, for example, several years down the road. Think about your future and know that your current actions will impact it.

Keeping your accounts from going into a collections status is a relatively easy process. If you can't afford to make the full payment due, contact the creditor and try to negotiate an alternative payment schedule. People who get themselves into financial trouble often tend to ignore the problems until they become huge legal problems. Simply by taking a responsible approach, paying what you can and working with your creditors, you can almost always keep your delinquent accounts out of collections, which will protect your credit and save you a fortune.

It's true that your creditors want to be paid in a timely manner. However, most also understand that people sometimes run into financial problems. You'll find that by communicating with your creditors and demonstrating good faith by making at least minimum monthly payments, the creditors will be understanding and try to help keep you from destroying your credit.

☆ ☆ **WARNING** ☆ ☆

Paying off a collection account will *not* automatically remove that negative trade line from your credit report. Your credit score will still suffer.

The easiest and most straightforward thing you can do to protect your credit report and credit score (or begin repairing it) is simply to pay your bills on time. It's that easy!

Strategy 2. Keep Your Credit Card Balances Low

The fact that you have credit cards impacts your credit score. Likewise, your payment history on those credit card accounts also impacts your score. Another factor that's considered in the calculation of your credit score is your credit card balances. Having a balance that represents 35 percent or more of your overall available credit limit on each card will actually hurt you, even if you make all of your payments on-time and consistently pay more than the minimum due. If you have a $1,000 credit limit on a credit card, ideally, you want to maintain a balance of less than $350, and make timely monthly payments on the balance that are above the required monthly minimums.

Demonstrate (through your credit history) that you're actively reducing your balances, while properly and responsibly utilizing your credit cards. Depending on your personal situation, it could make sense to spread your credit card debt over three, four, or five cards, while keeping your balance on each of them below that 35 percent of the total credit limit mark, as opposed to maxing out one credit card. If you do this, make timely payments on each card and keep them all in good standing. Managing your credit card debt appropriately

---

TIP

Need help making financial calculations related to your credit cards? You can utilize a free, online credit card debt calculator at www.BankRate.com.

---

will not only keep your score from dropping, it could also give it a boost.

Deciding to spread your credit card debt among several cards might help your credit score, however, before adopting this strategy, calculate the interest you'll be paying and compare interest rates between cards. In some cases, you may save money by consolidating your credit card balances onto one low-interest card, as opposed to having that same balance spread over several higher interest bearing cards. Do the math to help you make the decision and take the action that's best for you.

Use the worksheet in Figure 5.1 to help you manage your credit card debt, decide whether to consolidate your balances, and understand the cost of maintaining the debt over time. Some of the information you'll need to complete this worksheet can be found on your monthly credit card statements.

Strategy 3. Having a Good History Counts, So Don't Close Unused Accounts

One of the factors considered when calculating your credit score is the length of time you've had the credit established with each creditor. You are rewarded for having a positive, long-term history with each creditor, even if the account is inactive or not used. The longer your positive credit history is with each creditor, the better.

Knowing this, avoid closing older and unused accounts. If you have a handful of credit cards you never use, instead of

FIGURE 5.1: **CREDIT CARD MANAGEMENT WORKSHEET**

Credit Card Name	Account Number	Interest Rate	Credit Limit	Target Balance (35% of the credit limit)	Current Balance	Monthly Minimum Payment	Actual Monthly Payment	Monthly Interest Paid

closing the accounts, simply put the credit cards in a safe place and forget about them. Although you don't want to have too many open accounts, having five or six credit card accounts open, even though you only actually use two or three cards can be beneficial. Likewise, if you have a five-year car loan, for example, showing three, four, or five years of positive payment history (with no late or skipped payments), will benefit you.

☆ ☆ **WARNING** ☆ ☆

Closing an account does not remove the information from your credit report. The trade line for that account will remain on your credit reports for seven years (or longer), but it will reflect the action taken to close the account and state whether the account was paid in full, settled, or sent to collections.

Strategy 4. Only Apply for Credit When It's Needed, Then Shop for the Best Rates on Loans and Credit Cards

If you're in the market for a bunch of new appliances or other big-ticket items, it's common for consumers to walk into a retailer and be offered a discount and a good financing deal on a large purchase, if they open a charge or credit card account with that retailer. Before applying for that store's credit card, read the fine print. Determine what your interest rate will be and what fees are associated with the card.

Next, only apply for new credit if you absolutely need it. Applying for a retail store card you're going to use once or twice, when you could just as easily use an existing credit card, might not be the best idea. Applying for and obtaining multiple new credit cards (including store credit cards) within a several month period will be detrimental to your credit score. Unless you can save a significant amount of money on your purchase over time and can justify accepting a reduction in your credit score, don't apply for credit you don't actually need.

Strategy 5. Separate Your Accounts after a Divorce

During a marriage, it's common for a couple to obtain joint credit card accounts and co-sign for various types of loans. Coming into the marriage, the information on each person's credit report and their credit score will eventually impact their spouse, especially when new joint accounts are opened or a spouse's name is added to existing accounts. Consolidating all of your accounts once married makes record-keeping easier. If a couple gets divorced, however, this can create a whole new set of credit-related challenges.

First, understand that just because you obtain a legal divorce, it does *not* release one or both people from their financial obligations when it comes to paying off a joint account. As long as both names appear on the account, both parties are responsible for it.

☆ ☆ **WARNING** ☆ ☆

Even if a judge orders one person in the marriage to take full responsibility for a specific debt, such as a mortgage, car loan, or credit card bills, as long as it remains a joint account with both names appearing on the account, both parties remain financially responsible for it as far as the creditors and credit reporting agencies are concerned. Thus, if your ex-spouse pays a bill late or skips a payment, if that account is also in your name, it will be negatively reflected on your credit reports as well.

TIP

Be sure to close or separate all joint accounts after a divorce is finalized. This can be done by calling each creditor directly. You should also follow up the request in writing and make sure you receive confirmation that the change to the account has been made. Until all accounts are closed or separated, be sure to make on-time payments to all joint accounts. Remember, even one missed or late payment will show up on both of your credit reports and remain there for seven years.

As your divorce proceedings move forward, be sure to pay off and close all joint accounts, or have one person's name removed from each account, meaning only one person will remain responsible for it.

It will probably become necessary for one or both parties in the marriage to re-establish their independent credit. When doing this, start off slowly and build up your independent credit over a few years. Immediately applying for a handful of new credit cards, a new car loan, and/or a new mortgage within a short period of time after your divorce won't help to improve your credit report and credit score. Try to spread out new credit card acquisitions and new loans by at least six months each.

TIP

Depending on your situation, in order to re-establish your credit, it may be necessary to find a cosigner, such as a family member or close friend. Remember, when someone cosigns a credit or loan application, they're taking on equal responsibility for the debt you incur. If you make late payments, default on the loan, or skip payments, it will be reflected on your credit report as well as your cosigner's credit report and negatively impact both of your credit scores. As you're establishing or rebuilding your credit, it becomes more important than ever to pay all of your bills on time.

In the event of a spouse's death, creditors can not automatically remove the deceased person's name from the joint account and make the debt the sole responsibility of the living spouse. It will be necessary to contact each creditor separately. In some cases, the widow or widower may need to reapply for the credit card or loan as an individual borrower. Keep in mind that several of the credit reporting agencies regularly update their records using information provided by the Social Security Administration. As a result, joint accounts that include someone who is deceased will be flagged when the creditors are notified.

Strategy 6. Correct Inaccuracies in Your Credit Reports and Make Sure Old Information Is Removed

One of the fastest and easiest ways to quickly give your credit score a boost is to carefully review all three of your credit reports and correct any erroneous or outdated information that's listed. If you spot incorrect information, you can initiate

TIP

In order to have negative information removed from your credit report after initiating a dispute, you must be able to show that the negative information is inaccurate.

a dispute and potentially have it corrected or removed within 10 to 30 days. See Chapter 4 for details on how to initiate a dispute with a creditor or the credit reporting agencies.

Strategy 7. Avoid Excess Inquiries

Every time you apply for a credit card or any type of loan, a potential creditor will make an inquiry with one or more of the credit reporting agencies (Experian, Equifax, or TransUnion). This inquiry information gets added to your credit report and will typically remain listed for two years. For one year, however, the inquiry will slightly reduce your credit score. If you have multiple inquiries in a short period of time, this can dramatically reduce your credit score.

Keep in mind, when shopping for a mortgage or car loan, it's permissible to have multiple inquiries for the same purpose within a 30- to 45-day period, without those multiple

TIP

If you know you'll be applying for a mortgage or car loan within the next six months, do not apply for any other types of loans or credit cards in the interim. Excessive inquiries in a short period of time will lower your credit score and decrease your chances of getting approved.

inquiries hurting your credit score. In this situation, the multiple inquiries will be counted as one single inquiry.

Strategy 8. Avoid Bankruptcy, if Possible

There are a lot of misconceptions about the pros and cons of filing for bankruptcy if you encounter serious financial problems. In terms of your credit report and credit score, filing for bankruptcy is one of the absolute worst things you can do. If your credit score hasn't already plummeted as a result of late payments, missed payments, and defaults, when the bankruptcy is listed on your credit report, you will notice a large and immediate drop in your credit score. Furthermore, that bankruptcy will continue to plague your credit report for up to ten years.

For most people, bankruptcy does not offer an easy way out of their financial responsibilities or offer a quick fix. Instead, you're setting yourself up for long-term financial difficulties, because obtaining any type of credit or loans in the future will be significantly more difficult. Many mortgage brokers (and lenders) and car loan financing companies will automatically reject applicants with bankruptcies listed on their credit reports.

If you do file for bankruptcy, the best thing you can do is slowly rebuild your credit by paying all of your bills on time from that point forward, with no exceptions. Rebuilding your credit in this situation will mostly likely take years, with no quick fixes available.

☆ ☆ **WARNING** ☆ ☆

Just filing bankruptcy papers with the court is enough for it to negatively impact your credit report and credit score. Even if your bankruptcy papers are rejected by the court, the negative information will still appear on your credit report within the "Public Records" section, and that will impact your credit score.

☆ ☆ **WARNING** ☆ ☆

Filing for bankruptcy does not wipe clean all of your debt. You will still be responsible for alimony, child support, student loans, and taxes, for example.

Strategy 9. Avoid Consolidating Balances onto One Credit Card

Unless you can save a fortune in interest charges by consolidating balances onto one credit card, this strategy should be avoided. One reason to avoid this is that maxing out your credit card will detract from your credit score, even if you make on-time payments. Assuming the interest rate calculations make sense, you're better off distributing your debt over several low-interest credit cards. An alternative is to pay off high-interest credit card balances using another type of debt consolidation loan or by refinancing your mortgage with a cash-out option. See Chapter 7 for more information about debt consolidation options.

Strategy 10. Negotiate with Your Creditors

Contrary to popular belief, your creditors aren't your enemies (at least they don't have to be). Your creditors are in business. The nature of business dictates that they earn a profit. When you don't pay your bills, that impacts a creditor's ability to do business and impacts its bottom line. Many creditors are willing to be understanding of difficult financial situations and short-term financial problems, especially if you openly communicate with them in a timely manner.

In other words, instead of skipping a handful of payments or defaulting on a loan, contact the creditor as soon as a problem arises and negotiate some form of resolution that's acceptable and within your financial means. Forcing a creditor to turn your debt over to a collection agency will simply cause you bigger problems in the future because many collection agencies are relentless when it comes to recovering money. Furthermore, the negative information that's placed on your credit report will have a long-term negative impact on your credit score.

Depending on the level of your financial difficulties, your creditors may be willing to do one or more of the following things to assist you, assuming you make the effort and show good faith in contacting them to discuss your situation:

- Reduce your interest rate.
- Reduce your monthly minimum payment.

- Waive extra finance charges and late fees.
- Allow you to skip one or more monthly payments (and extend the length of the loan).
- Close the account and allow you to make affordable payments to slowly reduce the outstanding balance over time.
- Close the account and accept a settlement for less than the amount you actually owe.

TIP

Although you can easily negotiate with creditors on your own behalf, to learn more about what's possible to rectify or improve your situation before it gets too far out of control, consider seeking help from a professional credit counselor. In the past, accepting help from a credit counselor was detrimental to your credit report and credit score. *This is no longer the case.* For information about credit counseling, contact the National Foundation for Consumer Credit at (800) 388-2227. From this nonprofit organization, which has more than 1,450 offices throughout the country, you can receive low-cost or free guidance that can help you work with your creditors and develop a realistic budget for yourself based on your personal situation. Chapter 7 offers more information about credit counseling services and options available to consumers.

- Allow you to refinance the loan at a lower interest rate and/or for a longer term to reduce your monthly payments.

☆ ☆ **WARNING** ☆ ☆

Simply ignoring a debt, closing an account (or allowing an account to be closed by a creditor for nonpayment), or moving without providing a creditor with your new address will not cause the outstanding debt to disappear. In many cases, the longer you hold off paying your debts, the more you'll spend in interest fees, late fees, legal fees, and other types of penalties.

Avoiding Credit Repair Scams

There's a big difference between "credit repair," "debt consolidation," and "credit counseling." Credit repair services are typically a scam. Companies falsely advertise that for a fee, it will have accurate, but negative information removed from your credit report, which will quickly boost your credit score. These services don't work and in many cases are scams designed to prey on people suffering from financial difficulties. Only the credit reporting agencies or the actual creditor can remove information from your credit report. For example, the BankRate.com web site (www.bankrate.com/brm/news/advice/19980720c.asp) features an article entitled "Credit

Repair Scams," in which Jodie Bernstein, the director of the Federal Trade Commission's Bureau of Consumer Protection in Washington, DC, is quoted as saying, "While there are legitimate, not-for-profit credit counseling services, the FTC has never seen a legitimate credit repair company."

Unless you negotiate well with your creditors and pay off outstanding debts, it is virtually impossible to have negative (but accurate) information removed from your credit report. Furthermore, rebuilding your credit and boosting your credit score is a process that takes months, often years. If you see a "credit repair" service advertised, proceed with extreme caution before utilizing this type of service.

Debt consolidation involves taking out a new, larger loan at one predetermined interest rate, so that you can pay off multiple overdue outstanding debts that maybe charging much higher interest rates. Assuming you obtain a debt consolidation loan from a legitimate company, this can be an excellent way to begin rebuilding your credit and fixing financial problems. There are, however, debt consolidation loan companies that aren't legitimate or that charge exorbitant fees or interest rates. Make sure you fully understand the type of loan you are applying for and what your responsibilities are before proceeding. Consulting with a personal financial planner, accountant, credit counselor, or attorney before moving forward with a debt consolidation loan is an excellent strategy.

Credit counseling is a service that teaches you how to better manage your finances and offers negotiation with creditors on your behalf to help you regain your financial stability and rebuild your credit. There are often fees associated with credit counseling services, even if the organization you work with is a nonprofit corporation.

Some companies advertised as "credit counseling services" are really debt consolidation loan companies offering high-interest (and/or high fee) debt consolidation loans. Consumer beware! Make sure the debt consolidation firm you choose to work with is reputable. The National Foundation for Consumer Credit Counseling (800-388-2227, www.nfcc.org) is an excellent place to start your search for a reputable and affordable credit counseling service.

CHAPTER 6

Managing Your
Credit and Planning for Your Future

WHAT'S IN THIS CHAPTER

➢ Summarizing your credit situation.

➢ Ways to reduce your "cost of credit."

➢ Credit report and credit score considerations when applying for a mortgage.

➢ Applying for a car loan.

➢ Applying for credit cards.

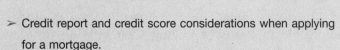

Understanding Your Current Credit Situation and Determining Your Credit Worthiness

Simply by analyzing your credit and money management skills, you can develop a general idea of your personal financial situation and where it's headed in the future. You already know if you have money in the bank, a steady income, and whether you can cover your bills each month (with hopefully at least a little left over for recreation and savings). However, few people truly understand their credit situations. When they apply for loans or credit cards, they're surprised to learn that their credit scores are much lower than they anticipated.

The information on your credit report tracks your credit management habits, such as how much you owe, your on-time payment history (or lack thereof), and who your creditors are. This has little to do with how much money you have in the bank, your income, the value of your assets, or your overall net worth. Simply by making a few late payments or mismanaging your credit, for example, even a multi-millionaire can have negative information on their credit report, which in turn causes their credit score to drop. At the same time, someone in a much lower income bracket could be much more responsible in terms of paying their bills on time and not overextending by using credit cards, resulting in an excellent credit score.

You already know that the more negative information that's added to your credit report over time, the worse your credit score will be. A low credit score eventually costs money because it keeps you from qualifying for prime rate mortgages and loans, as well as obtaining low-interest credit cards with few fees.

Your Current Credit Situation

The first step toward proper credit management involves taking an inventory of your current credit situation and analyzing how well you're utilizing your credit in your everyday

TIP

Based on your credit score and information on your credit report, you may qualify for lower interest loans and credit cards than what you already have. Reducing the rate of interest you're currently paying on your mortgage, car loan, home equity loan, and credit cards could save you hundreds or even thousands of dollars each month. Assuming your credit is average or above (and your credit score is at least 650 to 700), refinancing your current mortgage can be a quick way to cut expenses if you quality for a lower interest rate. In fact, based on what current rates are, you could save money immediately by paying a lower interest rate, plus change your 30-year fixed mortgage to a 15- or 20-year fixed rate mortgage. You could also potentially take cash from the equity in your home to pay off high-interest credit card debt to save additional money.

life. Are you paying too much interest on your mortgage? Could you qualify for a better deal based on your current credit score? Are you using your credit cards the best way possible to ensure you're not overpaying interest and you're not damaging your credit score? Are you maintaining a good reputation as a credit-using consumer by paying all of your bills on time?

The worksheet in Figure 6.1 will help you see how much you're relying on credit in your everyday life and assist you in developing ways to cut your costs by better utilizing the credit you already have available. Obviously, what you want to avoid is relying too heavily on credit to sustain your current standard of living, especially by constantly increasing your credit card debt in order to stay afloat.

If you're actively using high-interest credit cards and maintaining a significant balance on these cards, applying for credit cards with a lower interest rate and lower fees and then transferring your balances to those cards will also save you money each month. Shop around for the lowest interest bearing credit cards you can qualify for and then consider transferring your balances to them. (At the same time, develop a strategy to pay off or reduce your credit card debt, not just move it around.)

Some people realize a bit too late that their credit management skills are awful. In the process of realizing this, they rack up a significant amount of credit card debt, and have a series of other high-interest loans. When they finally get around to calculating how much of their monthly income they're spending on paying down their debt and on interest charges, they realize that something needs to be done. In many cases, once you've acquired a significant level of debt that's racking up high-interest charges each month, applying for a debt consolidation loan is a quick and relatively easy way to combine multiple high interest loans into one single lower interest loan. Doing this can help you reduce your monthly expenses and protect your credit score from dropping as a result of late payments or high credit card balances. To see if a debt consolidation loan (or refinancing your home and taking cash out to pay off debt) makes sense, utilize a free Debt Consolidation Loan Calculator, like the one found at LowerByBills.com.

By applying for credit or loans only when you actually need them, shopping around for the best deals you can qualify for, then paying your bills on time, you'll stay in a much better financial situation and be able to protect your credit reputation and credit score. Even if you don't need a mortgage, car loan, student loans, a home equity loan, or credit cards right now, consider what your needs will be three, five, or ten years down the road. The mistakes you make when managing your credit today (or the mistakes you've already made) will directly impact your ability to obtain credit in the future.

If you're single, working full time, and enjoying the dating process, it's hard to imagine that in a few years, you might want to settle down, buy a home, and start a family. This could mean that you'll need a mortgage and perhaps a car loan. Maybe you'll decide that before getting married that you want to go back to school to earn an advanced degree and will need student loans to pay for the education. By damaging your credit today, you run the real risk of not having the credit you'll need available in the future. Unfortunately, a lack of credit could prevent you from realizing your personal and financial goals and dreams.

Beware! Many Things Can Hurt Your Credit Score

Although paying your bills on time and properly managing your credit will help you maintain a high credit score, unfortunately, there's a long list of things that can negatively impact your credit score or keep you from being approved for a loan or having a credit card application approved. Just some of the potentially negative actions that people often take include:

- Having the amount owed on accounts be too high.
- Being delinquent on one or more accounts.
- Not allowing enough time to pass since your most recent account(s) were opened.
- The length of your revolving credit history is too short.
- Allowing the proportion of loan balances to total loan amounts become too high.
- Allowing the proportion of your balances to credit limits become too high on credit card (revolving) accounts.

- The time since one or more late payments is too short.
- The total amount owed on credit cards (revolving accounts) is too high.
- Causing negative information to appear in the Public Records section of your credit reports.
- Having too few bank revolving accounts (major charge cards as opposed to store credit cards).
- Having too few of your accounts show up as "Paid As Agreed" on your credit reports.
- Having too many accounts with balances.
- Having too many bank or national revolving accounts.
- Having too many consumer finance accounts (retail store credit cards).
- Having too many new accounts opened in the last 12 months.
- Having too many of your accounts show late payments.
- Having too many recent inquiries in the last 12 months.
- You have no recent revolving balances or not a well-established credit history.
- You have one or more accounts that have been turned over to collections or that have been charged off.
- You have too many 30-, 60-, 90- or 120-day past due accounts.
- You have too many revolving accounts (credit cards).
- Your account payment history is too new and the new creditors or lenders haven't yet provided enough information to the credit reporting agencies.

Do you have one or more credit cards with a balance that's more than 50 percent of your credit limit? Are the balances growing each month? If so, you're probably relying too heavily on credit card usage. Unless you're using the cards and paying off the balance for new purchases at the end of each billing cycle, or paying down your debt instead of causing it to grow, your spending habits probably need to change in order to protect your future stability in the near future and preserve your credit score. Remember, your credit score will be negatively impacted by high credit card balances, the overutilization of your credit cards, and any late payments you make. One of the first things people do when they run into a financial problem is rely on their credit cards to bail them out. This can be a quick fix for one or two months, but beyond that, credit card debt can easily get out of control to the point that it's extremely difficult to recover. Thus, the initial financial problem you experienced becomes significantly worse.

If you want to determine your actual FICO Score quickly, but don't want to pay for the scores from all three credit reporting agencies, you can call any mortgage broker and ask them to pre-qualify you for a mortgage. One of the first steps they'll take is obtaining your actual FICO Scores and copies of your credit report, which you can then request copies of. Although one inquiry will appear on your credit report, you will get a realistic picture of what actual lenders and creditors are actually seeing when they evaluate your credit report(s) and credit score(s).

Based on your current credit score and by doing a bit of research, you can compare the interest rates you're paying now on various types of loans and credit cards with the interest rates you could qualify for. To determine the current interest rates you could qualify for on a mortgage, car loan, or other types of loans, based on your current credit score and where you live, visit MyFICO.com and click on the "Loan Calculator" icon. Another excellent resource is LowerMy Bills.com.

By answering about 20 questions about your use of credit and your credit history, the free FICO Score Estimator, available from BankRate.com is an excellent tool for estimating your current FICO Score or predicting what could happen to your score based on various actions you take in the future, like applying for additional loans or making late payments.

As you complete the following worksheet (Figure 6.1), focus on calculating your loan and credit-related expenses for one month. Choose the most recent month possible and be sure to utilize all of your most recent statements and financial records.

The worksheet in Figure 6.1 will help you determine what your credit situation is like now, and then assist you in developing a game plan so you can better plan for your financial future (while at the same time, protecting your credit score). Start by determining what your credit score (more importantly your FICO Score) is today.

FIGURE 6.1: **CREDIT UTILIZATION WORKSHEET**

Current Experian FICO Score: _____

Current Equifax FICO Score: _____

Current TransUnion FICO Score: _____

Current Mortgage and Home Equity Credit Line Information

Lender	Loan Description (Example: 15-Year, Fixed-Rate)	Interest Rate (%)	Monthly Payment	Duration	Number of Months/Years Remaining

Total monthly payment: $ _____

Interest paid this month: $ _____

Current Car Loan Information

Lender	Loan Description	Interest Rate (%)	Monthly Payment	Duration	Number of Months/Years Remaining

Total monthly payment: $ _____

Interest paid this month: $ _____

FIGURE 6.1: CREDIT UTILIZATION WORKSHEET, CONT.

Current Student Loan(s)

Lender	Loan Description	Interest Rate (%)	Monthly Payment	Duration	Number of Months/Years Remaining

Total monthly payment: $ _____

Interest paid this month: $ _____

Current Credit and Charge Card Balances and Information

Credit Card Name	Credit Limit	Interest Rate (%)	Minimum Monthly Payment	Actual Monthly Payment	Annual Fees and Other Charges	Current Balance

Total monthly payment: $ _____

Interest paid this month: $ _____

FIGURE 6.1: CREDIT UTILIZATION WORKSHEET, CONT.

Other Revolving Credit (such as Store Credit Cards, Gas Station Cards, etc.)

Credit Card Name	Credit Limit	Interest Rate (%)	Minimum Monthly Payment	Actual Monthly Payment	Annual Fees and Other Charges	Current Balance

Total monthly payment: $ _____

Interest paid this month: $ _____

Other Outstanding Debts

Type of Debt	Creditor/ Lender	Amount Owed	Interest Rate	Monthly Payment

Total monthly payment: $ _____

Interest paid this month: $ _____

> **TIP**
>
> Simply by entering your current credit card balances, interest rates, minimum monthly payments (usually 2 to 2.5 percent of the total balance), your credit limits and your total balances for each card into the Credit Card Optimizer that's available at the MyFICO web site (www.myfico.com/CreditEducation/Calculators/CardOptimizer.aspx), you can instantly determine the best way to distribute your credit card debt between your various credit cards in order to reduce your interest and monthly payments, while still working to pay off the balances. You can enter information on up to five credit card accounts. This is a quick way to determine how much you could save simply by transferring your balances between cards.

Based on the information you entered into this worksheet for a specific month, you can see how your money is being spent and how much your credit is costing you in terms of fees and interest charges. Be sure to add in any late fees, over-limit fees or other types of penalties you've had to pay. This worksheet focuses exclusively on loans and credit that you're utilizing. Now, incorporate this information into your comprehensive personal or family budget to determine your overall financial situation and stability.

Using a software package, such as Microsoft Money Standard 2006 or Intuit's Quicken Basic 2006, is an easy way to create and manage a personal or family budget and better manage your use of available credit. Quicken Basic 2006 ($29.95) is a PC-based program. For more information, visit www.quicken.com. Microsoft Money Standard 2006 ($29.95) is another popular and comprehensive personal money management program that's easy-to-use and requires little financial knowledge to operate. For details, visit www.microsoft.com/money.

After you've completed the credit utilization worksheet, consider steps you can begin taking right away to lower your debts, reduce your interest rates, and more rapidly pay down the outstanding balances.

Reducing the Costs Associated with Credit

As a consumer, utilizing the credit you qualify for has long-term costs associated with it. These costs come in the form of interest and fees. If you don't pay your bills on time, late payments, additional penalties, and even legal fees may be added to your debt, causing the total amount owed to increase dramatically. The following strategies for lowering the costs associated with credit can be used to better manage any type of loan or credit card.

On an ongoing basis, pay more than what's required as your minimum monthly payment. Even an "overpayment" of a few dollars per month will add up over time, work toward reducing your balance, and reduce the amount you spend on interest fees. For example, if you have a $200,000, 20-year fixed rate mortgage, with an interest rate of 7.5 percent, your monthly payment would be $1,611. If you paid an additional $135 per month (approximately one-twelfth of one monthly payment), you'd pay off the entire mortgage three years and two months faster and save over $34,048 in interest. You can use the Mortgage Payoff Calculator found at MyFICO.com web site to see how the numbers work out based on your own situation (www.myfico.com/CreditEducation/Calculators/MortgagePayoff.aspx). This strategy can work for any type of interest-bearing loan you're trying to pay off, assuming the principal doesn't continue to increase due to new purchases on credit cards, for example.

When it comes to credit card debt, one way to begin reducing your balances and pay off your debt faster than you would if you simply pay the minimum due each month, is to take a two-step approach. First, focus on paying off your highest interest credit cards. Then, when a balance is paid in full, apply the same amount of money you were previously allocating to pay off that higher interest credit card toward paying the credit card with the next highest interest rate. Keep this process up until all of your cards are paid off. This is referred to as "rolling down" your credit card debt. For a calculator you can use to enter your own credit card information to see first-hand how this system works, go to: www.myfico.com/CreditEducation/Calculators/DebtRolldown.aspx.

Before applying for any type of loan or credit card, shop around for the best possible deals. When it comes to a mortgage, there are literally thousands of mortgage brokers offering a wide range of different types of mortgages you could potentially qualify for. Car loans, credit cards, home equity loans, and even student loans also offer a wide range of options. Always shop around for the lowest interest rates and best offers you can qualify for, even if it means talking to multiple lenders and exploring different options.

In terms of credit cards, you ideally want to find cards that offer a low annual percentage rate (APR), you'll see cards offering an APR of 7 percent or lower and cards offering an APR upwards of 30 percent, no annual fee, a low introductory rate, a special low balance transfer rate (if you plan to utilize this), no account activation fee, and some type of reward or cash back for using the card. There are several web sites you can visit to help you comparison shop for the best credit card deals, then apply for the cards that make the most sense for you. Remember, applying for too many credit cards too quickly can hurt you in the eyes of the credit reporting agencies and decrease your chances for approval. Applying for one new card every six to 12 months (or longer), and keeping each account current is important.

If you already have accumulated a large credit card debt using high-interest credit cards, consider some type of consolidation loan and develop a financial plan that keeps you from relying on credit cards for future purchases or to cover your everyday living expenses.

When you're in the market for a major appliance, expensive consumer electronics, jewelry, or some other high-ticket item, think twice before applying for a store credit card. Many retailers entice customers with a special introductory rate if they apply for and ultimately use a new store credit card account to finance a large purchase. The problem is, if you read the fine print in the Card Holder Agreement provided by the lender or card issuer, that special offer isn't always so special. If you're offered one year of interest-free financing, what happens on the 366th day? What will the interest rate be then? Will the interest that accrued over that first year be added to the balance due? What additional finance charges and fees will apply? You'll often discover that what seemed like an awesome deal can become an extremely high-interest loan after the initial special offer expires. It could make more sense to make the purchase using a low-interest credit card as opposed to a store credit card. If, however, you plan to pay off the entire purchase within the time period when zero percent interest and no finance charges are being charged, applying for that store credit card could make sense, providing the additional inquiry, new credit card account, and the added balance won't impact your credit score too negatively.

Financing a new or used car is another opportunity to save money, if you shop around for the best possible deals. If you complete a car loan application at a new or used car dealership, they'll typically shop the application to a variety of lenders, based on your credit score. The dealer might not always find you the best deal, however, especially if your credit score is below average. In addition to shopping for a loan through dealerships, visit a few different banks and credit unions, plus see what rates are available from lenders online. If your credit score is extremely low, you could potentially save a fortune in interest charges if you have someone with good credit co-sign the loan. Remember, during a 30- to 45-day period, you can have an unlimited number of inquiries on your credit report from car loan lenders, so shopping around won't hurt your credit score. When negotiating with a car dealership over the financing terms for your car, there's almost always room for negotiation.

Credit Report and Credit Score Considerations When Applying for a Mortgage

Buying a home is probably one of the largest expenses you'll incur in your lifetime. Most people don't have several hundred thousand dollars or more lying around in their savings accounts, so to afford a new home or condo, it's necessary to obtain a *mortgage*.

Mortgage. A mortgage is a long-term loan that's secured by the collateral of a specific real estate property. The borrower is obliged to make a predetermined series of payments to cover the principle, interest, and any related fees.

In the past, a typical mortgage was for a fixed period, such as 15, 20, or 30 years, and had a fixed interest rate throughout the entire life of the mortgage. This is referred to as a *fixed rate* mortgage, usually acquired through a local bank. Depending on the deal, in order to obtain the fixed rate mortgage, the borrower may have been required to pay closing costs and points for the loan to be processed.

> **TIP**
>
> To see what the current rates are for various types of mortgages, one resource is Bankrate.com. Only people with excellent credit can typically qualify for these prime rates. People with average or below average credit can expect to pay significantly higher rates.

Although fixed rate mortgages are still a viable option for many borrowers, today there are literally dozens of different types of mortgage options available. There are *adjustable rate mortgages*, mortgages that start off as fixed but then become adjustable rate mortgages after a predetermined number of years, *FHA mortgages*, *VA mortgages*, *jumbo* loans, *interest-only* loans, and many others.

Deciding on the type of mortgage to apply for will be based on what you can qualify for based on information in your credit reports and your credit scores, what you can afford, how much money you can use as a down payment, what your long-term goals are, and personal preference.

Today, borrowers not only have a wide range of mortgage options, they can work with their local banks, credit unions, or financial institutions, or shop for the best mortgage deals by working with reputable mortgage brokers or even by doing some comparison shopping online. Ultimately, how much you pay for your mortgage and what interest rate you receive will be determined by how well you shopped and negotiated for the best deal, as well as information on your credit report, your credit score, and potentially your earning history.

Before you begin shopping around for a mortgage, develop a good understanding of your personal credit situation and find out your current FICO Score with each credit reporting agency. This will help you determine what types of mortgages you qualify for and at what rates. Also, consider what you can afford as a monthly mortgage payment and how much of a down payment you'll be able to make on the new home. With this information, talk to several reputable mortgage brokers and lenders and begin the pre-qualification and application processes.

The best way to find a reliable mortgage broker or lender is through a referral from someone you know. You can easily respond to an ad, a telemarketing call from a mortgage broker, or find a mortgage broker online, but you won't know the reputation or reliability of that broker. Finding someone who is extremely knowledgeable and willing to work with you to determine the best mortgage option based on your personal situation can save you thousands of dollars. Working with someone who isn't knowledgeable or who is dishonest could cost you a fortune in fees, interest, and other expenses.

Unfortunately, not all mortgage brokers are reputable, including companies you constantly see advertised on television or hear about on the radio. As you begin negotiating with the broker and you're offered a deal, get it in writing. Then, during each stage of the mortgage process, make sure the initially agreed to deal is being adhered to and that no fees have been added and the interest rate has not changed. A last-minute change just before your closing could cost you a lot of money or get you in a mortgage you're not happy with. Beware of bait and switch schemes, for which you're initially given an attractive offer, but after doing all of the paperwork associated with applying for a mortgage, the broker says, "Hey, I can't get you qualified for the loan we initially discussed, but if you sign right now, I can lock in this other loan, which is also a great deal." As you're negotiating with the lender or broker, make sure you understand all of the fees involves. The *Good Faith Estimate* and *Truth In Lending Disclosure* provided by the lender or broker will outline all of the fees and interest you will be responsible for. Read it carefully.

Don't Wait Until the Last Minute to Check Your Credit

Having a mortgage application accepted can be a somewhat time-consuming process, both for you and the broker or lender you're working with, especially if your credit rating is less than excellent or if you have other extenuating circumstances that relate to you being approved. One of the biggest pitfalls consumers run into when applying for a mortgage is discovering negative information on their credit reports, which have caused a much lower than expected credit score.

Because your credit score will directly impact the interest rate and mortgage deal you'll qualify for, it's important to go into the application process with the best credit reports possible. Two or three months before your begin applying for mortgages, review your credit report, have any errors corrected and, if possible, pay off any outstanding loans and debt. Do whatever you can to quickly boost your credit scores (using information and strategies offered in Chapters 4 and 5). Remember, it could take 30 to 60 days for information, such as a credit card balance that's been paid off, to be reflected on your credit report and impact your credit score.

In situations for which action needs to be taken quickly to change information on your credit report by working directly with your lenders or creditors, your mortgage broker will most likely be able to help you by providing a "rapid rescoring" service through a third party. Thus, if you fix an error on your report, make a payment to lower a credit card balance or

---

TIP

The guidelines described in this section for finding a mortgage broker and applying for a mortgage also apply to refinancing your mortgage and can apply to obtaining a home equity or home improvement loan.

> **TIP**
>
> If you get approved for a mortgage with less than excellent credit, you can spend the next few years rebuilding or improving your credit, then refinance your mortgage at a better rate in the future and save money in the long term.

pay off an outstanding debt, you can have that information positively reflected on your credit report (and your credit score) often within 72 hours, not 30 or more days. Utilizing a rapid rescoring service, however, can be extremely expensive. This fee can be avoided by working toward cleaning up your credit report several months before you begin the mortgage application process.

Waiting until the last minute to address credit report issues will often result in your not qualifying for the best prime mortgage rates. Although you could still qualify for a mortgage, the interest rate and fee structure won't be as attractive. Whether you have excellent credit or below average credit, finding and working with a reputable, friendly, and knowledgeable mortgage broker or lender will be extremely beneficial and could keep you from having to go through the hassle of refinancing your mortgage too soon (unless you choose to do this in order to qualify for a better rate).

Applying for Low Fee and Low Interest Credit Cards

Choosing the best credit card offer(s) to apply for requires careful shopping and comparisons between offers, especially if you have average or below average credit. Although many credit card issuers (such as Capital One, First Premier, Orchard Bank, and New Millennium Bank) will approve a credit card application from someone with a low credit score, the APR and fees associated with those credit cards will often be astronomical, and your credit limit will be very low.

For example, one credit card offer that targeted people with a below average credit score offered a 19.75 percent APR with a 25.75 percent cash advance APR, a 25.75 percent delinquency APR for purchases, and a 31.75 percent delinquency APR for cash advances. In addition, this particular card has a $150 annual fee, a $29 one-time account opening fee, and a $6.50 per month account maintenance fee. Additional fees associated with this card included a transaction fee of 5 percent for cash advances, a $35 late payment fee (in addition to the higher APR), and a $35 over-limit fee. According to the credit card issuer, "The delinquency APR will apply in the event that you do not pay the required minimum payment by its due date for two consecutive billing cycles or for any four billing cycles in any 12-month period."

This offer is a far cry from those 0 percent interest rates for one year and no annual fee credit cards offered to consumers with excellent credit. When shopping for credit cards, be sure to carefully read the Card Holder Agreement or Summary of Credit Terms to fully understand all of the fees and different APR rates associated with the card. Don't just read the special offer letter, advertisement, or headline and assume what's being offered is a great deal.

For someone who has a low credit score and a poor credit history, in order to reestablish credit and begin rebuilding their credit score, it is often necessary to take advantage of less-than-attractive credit card offers for a few years. When you pursue this option, however, make sure you're able to carefully manage your credit card usage to stay current and avoid any excess charges (late fees, etc.). See the Glossary for definitions of credit card terms.

Another way to establish or rebuild credit is to apply for one or two secured credit cards. These work just like any other major credit cards (Visa or Mastercard), however, your credit limit is determined directly by the amount of money you deposit into a special account provided by the card issuer. Thus, the credit card is secured by the money you have on deposit. A variety of fees apply to this type of card, but the benefit is that the accounts are reported to the credit reporting agencies as regular credit cards, so if you manage one or two of these accounts properly, you can begin rebuilding or establishing credit. (Secured credit cards are different from bank issued debit cards, which deduct money for purchases directly from your checking account. Secured credit cards are also different from prepaid Visa or Mastercard debit cards that require an advance payment, which determines your credit limit. These prepaid credit cards do not report to the credit reporting agencies.)

Shop Around for the Best Credit Card Deals

In addition to contacting your local bank, credit union, or financial institution, conduct your own credit card or secured credit card comparison shopping, using the following web sites:

- http://moneycentral.msn.com/banking/services/credit card.asp
- www.bankrate.com
- www.cardratings.com

TIP

College students first trying to establish credit can take advantage of a variety of special credit card offers. Proof of being a full-time student is required to take advantage of these offers. Credit card offers targeted specifically to college students are advertised on college campuses and are often mailed directly to college students. Remember, improperly managing these credit card accounts could destroy your credit rating and reduce your credit score, just as the improper use of any credit card would.

- www.creditcards.com
- www.creditcardscenter.com
- www.e-wisdom.com/credit_cards/chart.html
- www.lowermybills.com

☆ ☆ **WARNING** ☆ ☆

For each credit card you have, become familiar with the terms and fees listed within the Card Holder Agreement. Every credit card account will come with a different agreement and will have different fees and rates associated with it. Don't just read one Card Holder Agreement and assume it applies to all of your credit cards, even if you have multiple cards from the same bank, financial institution or card issuer.

Your Future Starts Now

If you know you'll someday (within the next seven to ten years) be purchasing a home and obtaining a mortgage, buying (or leasing) a car, need a new credit card, or be applying for any type of credit or loan, it will be necessary to have "good" or "excellent" credit. By determining what your credit situation is like right now, you can begin building, rebuilding, and better managing your credit so it will be available to you when you need it. Simply by avoiding common credit-related mistakes made by consumers, you can protect your credit rating. If, however, you have gotten yourself into an extremely bad credit situation, there is help for you! Be sure to read Chapter 7 for information about free or low-cost credit counseling services.

Getting the Help You **Need to Fix Your Credit Problems**

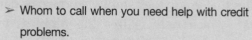

WHAT'S IN THIS CHAPTER

➢ Whom to call when you need help with credit problems.

➢ What credit counseling is and how it works.

➢ Working with a financial planner or accountant on an ongoing basis.

➢ Beware of credit repair scams.

➢ Debt consolidation loan options.

Solutions for People with Credit and Financial Problems

There are countless reasons people get themselves into serious debt, max out their credit cards, and simply run out of money. Some of these reasons include:

- Becoming a victim of theft or fraud
- Carelessness with money and spending habits
- Death of a loved one
- Getting laid off from a job
- Not developing a well-thought-out personal or family budget and then sticking to it
- Sudden illness or a medical emergency

Whatever the reason, people who find themselves experiencing serious financial problems often don't realize it until it's too late. Then, because the problem has gotten so big and out of control, these people don't know where to begin in terms of fixing the situation, so they simply ignore it or develop a sense of denial, which only causes the problem to get increasingly worse.

Whether it's the result of financial problems or the cause of them, what goes hand-in-hand with having personal financial problems is developing debt and poor credit. As you fall behind on monthly payments for loans and credit cards, negative information begins popping up on your credit reports. This leads to a steady reduction in your credit score, which causes the interest rates you're paying on your credit cards and loans to increase. Plus, when you attempt to apply for additional credit or loans, at first, you just pay more due to your lower credit score, but after some time passes, you discover you're unable to qualify for new loans and credit at all.

This is the point when many people discover they're in serious financial trouble and don't know where to turn or what to do. When you discover yourself experiencing any type of short- or long-term financial problems, it's important to begin dealing with them immediately to avoid much larger problems down the road.

For example, if you can't make your car loan payment in a given month, call the creditor and explain your situation and the reason. If the reason is valid, the lender will often work with you by extending the loan and allowing you to skip one or two payments, restructure or refinance the loan with a lower interest rate, waive interest fees or late charges, or work with you to develop a solution that will help keep you from experiencing further financial hardship.

Especially if you've recently lost your job, experienced a medical emergency, or have some other extenuating circumstance surrounding your personal and financial life, the trick to avoiding long-term credit and financial problems is to immediately contact your creditors and lenders and work with them. Don't allow bills to pile up as you skip payments and ponder what you're going to do, or just ignore the situation.

In the United States alone, there are countless people every month who begin experiencing serious financial and credit difficulties, yet don't know where to turn. If you're fortunate to have worked with an accountant, CPA (Certified Public Account), financial planner, or Certified Financial Planner (CFP) in the past that is familiar with your financial situation, this is definitely the type of financial expert to turn to now. Even if you've never worked with any type of accountant or financial planner in the past, if you can afford to hire one, even for a few hours, to review your current situation and recommend some solutions, this is the fastest and easiest way to begin seeking solutions to your financial and credit problems.

When seeking an accountant or financial planner, find someone with experience and expertise working with people in your situation, but beware of people advertising themselves as "credit repair experts." Find someone with some type of certification. For example, find a CPA instead of just an accountant. If you're seeking a financial planner, find someone who has earned his CFP certification. This will help guar-

---

TIP

The best way to find an accountant or financial planner is through a referral from someone you know. Otherwise, consider contacting a professional association, such as the Certified Financial Planner Board of Standards (www.cfp.com/search/).

---

antee that the person you ultimately hire is qualified, experienced, and reputable.

If you're experiencing credit problems, you could also seek guidance from a reputable credit counseling service. A financial planner can help you with all aspects of money management and budgeting. A credit counselor can:

- Advise you about managing your money and your use of credit
- Provide solutions and strategies for dealing with your current financial problems
- Assist you in creating a personalized plan to help you prevent future difficulties
- Help you negotiate with your creditors and lenders
- Develop and help you implement a Debt Management Plan (DMP) to bail yourself out of your financial predicament

When you begin working with a financial expert, whether an accountant, financial planner, or credit counselor, the personal and financial information you provide is typically kept confidential, unless you authorize the person you're working with to contact and negotiate with your creditors and lenders on your behalf.

Strategies for Finding a Qualified Financial Planner

In the United States, there are more than 50,000 CFPs. On its web site (www.cfp.com), the Certified Financial Planner

Board of Standards offers the following advice for finding a qualified financial planner to assist you in overcoming your financial and credit problems:

- *Know what you want.* Determine your general financial goals and/or specific needs (insurance policy analysis, estate planning, investment advice, college tuition financing, etc.) to better focus your search for a suitable financial planner.
- *Be prepared.* Read personal finance publications (*Worth, Money, SmartMoney, Kiplinger's Personal Finance,* etc.) to maximize your familiarity with financial planning strategies and terminology.
- *Talk to others.* Get referrals from advisors you trust, business associates, and friends. Or contact one of the financial planning membership organizations for a referral to a financial planner in your area.
- *Look for competence.* A number of specialty designations exist in the financial planning and services arenas. Choose a financial planning professional with the certification that indicates that he or she is ethical and has met standards of financial planning competency and has acquired the CFP certification.
- *Interview more than one planner.* Ask the planners to describe their educational backgrounds, experience and specialties, the size and duration of their practices, how often they communicate with clients, and whether an assistant handles client matters. Make sure you feel

comfortable discussing your finances with the planner you select.

- *Check the planner's background.* Depending on the financial planner's area of expertise, call the securities or insurance departments in your state regarding each planner's complaint record. Call CFP Board toll-free at (888) CFP-MARK or visit www.CFP.net to determine if a planner is currently authorized to use the CFP certification marks or has ever been publicly disciplined by the CFP Board.
- *Know what to expect.* Ask for a registration or disclosure statement (such as a Form ADV) detailing the planner's compensation methods, conflicts of interest, business affiliations, and personal qualifications.
- *Get it in writing.* Request a written advisory contract or engagement letter to document the nature and scope of services the planner will provide. You should also understand whether compensation will be fee- or commission-based, or a combination of both.
- *Reassess the relationship regularly.* Financial planning relationships are often long term. Review your professional relationship on a regular basis and ensure that your financial planner understands your goals and needs as they develop and change over time.

Credit Counselors Are Available to Help You

Many companies advertise credit counseling and credit repair services. Although you can assume that virtually all

---

TIP

If you need the help of a credit counselor, your first call should be to the National Foundation for Credit Counseling (800-388-2227, www.nfcc.org). You'll be provided with free information and have the opportunity to speak with a certified credit counselor who will charge you little or no money for the consultation.

---

companies that promote themselves as "credit repair" companies are not legitimate, it's harder to determine if a credit counseling service is reputable. Instead of responding to ads on late-night television or on the radio, for example, one of the best ways to find a reliable and reputable credit counseling service is to contact the National Foundation for Credit Counseling (800-388-2227, www.nfcc.org) for a referral in your area.

The National Foundation for Credit Counseling (NFCC) was founded in 1951 and is the county's largest and longest serving national nonprofit credit counseling organization. The NFCC's mission is to set the national standard for quality credit counseling, debt reduction services, and education for financial wellness through its member agencies. The NFCC's agencies have trained, certified credit counselors who offer low-cost and free educational information, management advice, and debt reduction services. NFCC members help more than two million consumers annually through nearly 1,000 agency offices nationwide.

According to the Debt Advice web site,

> *The NFCC offers consumers step-by-step counseling to become debt free. This is done by providing each consumer with an individualized plan to help them pay off their debt. If you've accumulated severe debt, the organization can help you establish a Debt Management Plan (DMP).*
>
> *According to the Debt Advice web site operated by the NFCC, "A DMP is a systematic way to pay down your outstanding debt through monthly deposits to the agency, which will then distribute these funds to your creditors. By participating in this program, you may benefit from reduced or waived finance charges and fewer collection calls. And when you have completed your payments, we'll help you reestablish credit . . . . A DMP is a carefully formulated,*

TIP

The NFCC operates an informative web site offering consumers tools and information to help them develop short and long-term strategies for fixing their credit problems. To learn more, visit Debt Advice.org (www.debtadvice.org).

---

monthly program that reduces your bills and consolidates them into one simple payment."

If you choose to participate in a DMP, the process of repaying your debt could take anywhere from 36 to 60 months. After negotiating with your creditors, a DMP can help you repay your debts in an organized and efficient way and lead you toward reestablishing your financial stability. The NFCC will work with you one-on-one by providing free or extremely affordable counseling services. The organization also offers free educational seminars through its regional offices.

The Debt Advice web site reports, "What sets the NFCC agencies apart from other nonprofit organizations is that it receives funding from sources besides its clients. As a result, while other credit counselors charge high start-up fees and monthly service charges, the NFCC's rates are extremely low and there are no hidden costs to immediately begin benefiting from the services offered."

Debt Management Plan (DMP). A credit counseling service can help you create and implement a formal and personalized debt management plan or DMP, which can be used to systematically pay off your debt over an extended period of time.

Because there are a significant number of companies and individuals that fraudulently pass themselves off as credit counselors in order to capitalize on the misfortune of people in severe debt, the Federal Trade Commission has developed a list of eight questions to help you determine if a particular credit counseling agency is reputable. These questions include:

1. *What services are offered?* A reputable credit counseling service will offer budget counseling and savings and debt management classes, plus be able to provide you with the services of someone who is trained and certified in consumer credit, money, and debt management. A credit counseling service should begin by discussing your personal situation with you, help you develop a personalized plan to solve your immediate money and credit problems, and then teach you how to avoid the recurrence of these problems in the future. During your first meeting with a credit counselor, be prepared to spend between 60 and 90 minutes analyzing your personal situation.

2. *Is the credit counselor licensed in your state to provide the services offered?* Many states require counselors to obtain a license before they're allowed to offer credit counseling, debt management plans, or other related services to consumers.

3. *Does the credit counseling service offer free information?* As a consumer looking to work with a credit counselor, you should never be charged for information about what services are offered by a specific company.

4. *Will you be required to sign a formal contract or written agreement with the credit counseling company?* Make sure

you never agree to pay for any services over the telephone. You should receive a written contract or agreement before being charged for credit counseling services or participating in a Debt Management Plan (DMP) coordinated by the credit counseling company.

5. *Does the credit counseling agency or service you're interested in working with have a good reputation with the Better Business Bureau and your state's Attorney General?* Determine if there have been any formal complaints filed against the company. From the Better Business Bureau's web site (www.bbb.org), you can search for complaints against a company and find contact information for your local BBB office. Keep in mind that even if you can't find any complaints against a specific company, that is not an absolute guarantee that the company is reputable.

6. *How much will the credit counseling services cost?* Be sure to obtain a detailed price quote in writing and make sure that all of the fees are actually listed within the quote. Determine if there are any up-front or start-up costs, monthly fees, or any other charges for the various services offered.

7. *How are the individual credit counselors paid?* Are they given a commission based on services you sign up for? According to the FTC, "If the organization will not disclose what compensation it receives from creditors, or how employees are compensated, go elsewhere for help."

> **TIP**
>
>
>
> The Federal Trade Commission publishes free booklets, including *Fiscal Fitness: Choosing A Credit Counselor* and *Knee Deep in Debt*, which can be obtained online at www.ftc.gov/credit or by calling (877) FTC-HELP. These booklets provide useful information if you're looking to hire a credit counselor, apply for a debt consolidation loan, or filing for bankruptcy.

8. *Will the information you provide to the credit counselor be kept confidential?* Who will have access to the personal and financial information you supply?

Debt Negotiation Service. Like a credit counseling company, a debt negotiation service will help you make contact with your specific creditors and negotiate on your behalf to help you pay off or settle your debt, depending on the circumstances.

Beware of Scams

As a consumer, you'll see many ads offering credit repair and fast and easy relief of debt. Many of these ads, however, are for scams. The FTC reports that some of the most common headlines to watch out for include: "Consolidate your bills into one monthly payment without borrowing," "STOP credit harassment, foreclosures, repossessions, tax levies and garnishments," "Keep Your Property," "Wipe out your debts! Consolidate your bills! How? By using the protection and assistance provided by federal law. For once, let the law work for you!" Services that utilize advertisements or sales literature which feature these or similar headlines should be avoided.

To help you choose a credit counseling or debt negotiation service to work with, the Federal Trade Commission has published a list of promises often made by disreputable companies who could be perpetuating some type of scam. If one or more of the following promises or claims are made, *do not* work with the company that makes them.

- The company or individual guarantees your unsecured debt can be erased or removed from your credit report and that the creditors you owe money to will simply go away.
- The company promises that unsecured debts can be paid off with pennies on the dollar.
- The company requires substantial monthly service fees and/or a start-up fee.
- The company demands a percentage of savings as payment.
- The company tells you to stop making payments to or communicating with your creditors.
- The company requires you to make monthly payments to them, rather than to your creditor, but you're not participating in a legitimate debt management plan (DMP).

- The company claims that creditors never sue consumers for nonpayment of unsecured debt.
- The company promises that using its system will have no negative impact on your credit report.
- The company claims it can remove negative, but accurate, information from your credit report.

Debt Consolidation

If you have multiple credit cards with balances and other types of high interest loans, debt consolidation involves taking out one (lower interest) loan and then using that money to pay off multiple other loans and credit cards. Not only will this allow you to pay just one monthly bill, it could save you a fortune in interest charges and help keep negative information from appearing on your credit report.

Debt consolidation is often used by people with multiple high-interest credit cards with high balances. However, it can also be used to help pay off student loans and other types of debt, because a debt consolidation loan will often carry with it a much lower interest rate than what you're currently paying.

There are several types of debt consolidation loans. Some people choose to refinance their mortgages and cash out some of their equity in their properties in order to pay off a handful of credit cards or other loans. You could also apply for a home equity loan or second mortgage, or apply for some other type of personal loan and use it for debt consolidation purposes. Another option is to apply for a low-interest credit card and transfer your high-interest credit card balances to that new card.

☆ ☆ **WARNING** ☆ ☆

Many debt consolidation loans require you to put up your home as collateral. Defaulting on the loan could cause a foreclosure (the loss of your home or property).

If used properly, a debt consolidation loan can be a powerful tool for regaining control over your debt, paying off past due accounts, and saving a lot of money in interest fees. Contact your financial institution, mortgage broker, bank, or financial planner for information about how a debt consolidation loan could potentially help you deal with your current financial or credit problems. Remember, this isn't a solution for everyone. Whether you can benefit from a debt consolidation loan will depend on your personal situation.

Some companies that offer debt consolidation loans or mortgage refinancing for debt consolidation purposes charge hidden fees, plus other fees in the form of "points" and closing costs. Or, they charge high interest rates, especially to borrowers with below average credit. Make sure you understand the type of loan you're being offered, what the rates and fees are, and determine that the loan you ultimately select will actually save you money after the consolidation process is complete. Understand exactly how the debt consolidation loan will benefit you, based on the situation you're currently in. Simply trading several high-interest (credit card) debts for one new high-interest debt isn't necessarily beneficial, unless it can improve your credit rating, bring you up-to-date with your creditors, allow you to pay off old debt, and help improve your credit score. Thus, in six months to one year, you'd qualify for a much lower interest loan and will have dramatically improved your credit situation.

Don't Be Afraid to Seek Help

If you find yourself in serious debt or experiencing major credit problems, whether it's due to circumstances beyond your control or poor money and credit management, don't be afraid to seek out help in order to properly fix your problems *before* they get too far out of control. There's no shame or need to be embarrassed about seeking out guidance from a certified, licensed, experienced, and reputable financial planner, accountant, or credit counselor. No matter how dire your situation is, however, don't become a victim of a scam by believing a company's lies that your financial or credit problems can be solved quickly and easily, without actually paying off your debt. Make sure you find someone who is trustworthy and knowledgeable and offers services you need and can afford.

Remember, even if you're in serious debt, there are organizations and credit counseling services that are willing and able to help you, either for free or for a very small fee. Seeking professional help with your financial problems could be one of the best investments you ever make, especially if you're willing to follow the advice that's offered and are able to eventually solve your financial and credit problems. There are few situations that are so bad that they can't eventually be fixed, even if it means filing for bankruptcy and rebuilding your financial stability and credit rating from scratch. Filing for bankruptcy, however, should only be considered as an absolute last resort and only after you've consulted with a credit counselor or personal finance expert.

Meet the
Credit Reporting Agency Gurus

WHAT'S IN THIS CHAPTER

➢ Indepth interviews with two credit experts, representing Experian and TransUnion, two major credit reporting agencies.

➢ Insider secrets about your credit report and credit score, directly from the credit reporting agencies.

➢ Expert strategies and tips for improving your credit, boosting your credit score, and managing your personal finances.

The Experts Speak Up

Throughout this book, you've been reading how important your credit report and credit score are as they relate to your financial well-being. In this chapter, you'll read exclusive interviews with experts on credit who share their personal and professional advice and reveal credit-related information that many consumers are unaware of.

As you read these interviews, keep in mind that the views expressed come directly from the experts and represent their personal or professional opinions. How you utilize this information is entirely up to you.

Lucy Duni
Director of Consumer Education
TrueCredit.com (TransUnion)

As you already know, TransUnion is one of the nation's three largest and most influential credit reporting agencies. TrueCredit.com is TransUnion's division that deals directly with consumer credit education and provides free and fee-based online services to consumers, such as the ability to order a copy of your credit report online or have your credit report monitored for changes or signs of identity theft. Three-in-one credit reports can also be ordered from True Credit.com. On this web site, you'll find a variety of easy-to-understand educational and credit management tools.

In this interview, Lucy Duni describes how credit reporting agencies like TransUnion work. She also provides valuable tips and strategies for managing your credit. You can find more information at www.TrueCredit.com.

What is a credit reporting agency and how do they work?

Lucy: There are three national credit reporting agencies. The creditors, such as lenders and credit card companies, report consumer payment information to the credit reporting agencies, which are a repository of information. Lenders then look to those repositories when they're considering lending money to a consumer. Basically, a credit reporting agency is a repository of information pertaining to a consumer's payment history. A credit report contains personal information, employment information, account information relating to creditors or lenders, public records and inquiry information. A credit report also contains contact information for every creditor listed, so a consumer can contact that creditor directly to pay off a debt, offer a settlement or correct an error.

How does someone go about getting erroneous information removed from their credit report?

Lucy: It's important that all information on a credit report be accurate, since negative information will remain on the report for upwards of seven years. If an item listed on your credit report is inaccurate, you can contact the three credit reporting agencies separately and the creditor itself and have that inaccurate information removed within 30

TIP

See Chapter 4 for step-by-step directions on how to contact the credit reporting agencies and your creditors to correct inaccurate information on your credit report.

days. If the negative information you want removed is accurate, however, you need to contact the creditor directly and work with them to resolve the dispute. It's at the creditor's discretion whether they wish to remove any correctly stated negative information on your credit report that they've added.

What is the process for getting incorrect information removed from a credit report?

Lucy: The process begins by obtaining a copy of your credit report and finding specific errors. Next, contact the creditor directly and attempt to resolve the dispute either over the phone or in writing. If that doesn't work, a consumer can dispute information on their credit report directly with the credit reporting agencies. This can be done online, by telephone or through the mail. If you're looking for quick results, attempting to contact the credit reporting agencies to correct your credit report online is the fastest method. Once you report an error, the credit reporting agency has 30 days to investigate the dispute, contact the creditor and correct the error if it exists. If your credit report contains personal factual data that's wrong, such as the spelling of your name or your address, you should contact the credit reporting agency directly to make those corrections. There is no charge to dispute inaccuracies on your credit report. While you can obtain a three-in-one credit report to review your information from all three credit reporting agencies, it is necessary to contact each of the three credit reporting agencies separately in order to correct an error that appears on each report. Remember, each credit reporting agency may have slightly different information.

Can anyone access my credit report?

Lucy: Any consumer can access their own credit report. Anytime a consumer applies for credit, that creditor can also access your credit report and credit score to help decide whether to grant you credit. Landlords, employers and other companies or individuals can also gain access to your credit report, but only if they first obtain your written consent.

How does the credit score relate to the credit report?

Lucy: The credit score is really what makes the credit report meaningful. It summarizes all of the factors that go into a credit report, including payment history, length of credit history and the types of accounts on the credit report. All of this information is combined into a complex mathematical formula. Positive information boosts your score, while negative information brings the score down. A credit score is designed to be a helpful tool to both creditors and consumers. It changes constantly. Different factors impact the credit score differently.

What are some simple things someone can do to boost their credit score quickly?

Lucy: There's really no such thing as a quick fix. There are, however, things you can do that will help boost your score more than others. The main thing that impacts your score is your payment history. If you know you'll be applying for a car loan in the next year, be sure to make on time payments starting as far in advance as possible. Six months or more of on-time payments, for example, will boost your score. Maxing out your credit cards will lower your score. Ideally, you want to keep the balances of your credit cards at or below 35 percent of your credit limit on an ongoing basis, in order to boost that aspect of your credit score. The length of your credit history, if the information is positive, will also boost your score. If you establish positive credit early on in your adult life, that will help. Another thing that can immediately decrease your credit score is having a bunch of credit inquiries added to your credit report. So, if you know you'll be applying for a car loan or mortgage in a few months, don't also apply for a handful of new credit cards or other types of loans.

If you're shopping for a great mortgage deal or a car loan, does it hurt your credit score to have multiple lenders access your credit report during this shopping process?

Lucy: No. Within a 30 to 45-day period, depending on the credit reporting agency, you can shop around for a mortgage or car, for example, and not have multiple inquiries lower your credit score. A handful of inquiries for a mortgage or car loan within a 30-day period will be grouped together and counted as just one inquiry.

Is information that appears on a three-in-one credit report identical to information that would be listed on a single credit report issued by one of the major credit reporting agencies?

Lucy: Yes. When you purchase a three-in-one credit report, it immediately gathers information from all three credit reporting agencies, but formats that data in one place, so it can be easily viewed. A three-in-one credit report is a simple and convenient tool for consumers to make reviewing their credit report easier. The alterative is to contact each credit reporting agency separately and obtain separate credit reports from each, then compare each item manually. While obtaining a single credit report from each credit reporting agency can be done for free once per year, it is necessary to purchase a three-in-one credit report. This

---

TIP

When you obtain a copy of your credit report for free, it does not include your corresponding credit score. The three credit reporting agencies typically charge for credit score information. See Chapter 2 for details on how to obtain your credit score from the three credit reporting agencies and how these scores are evaluated by mortgage companies, credit card companies, and other creditors and lenders.

---

can be done quickly and easily online, from a service like TrueCredit.com.

What are some of the biggest misconceptions consumers have about the credit reporting agencies and credit reports?

Lucy: One of the biggest misconceptions is that checking your own credit report will hurt your credit score. This is untrue. There are two types of inquiries. A *'hard inquiry'* comes from a creditor who checks your credit report when you apply for credit. This will impact your credit score. A *'soft inquiry,'* however, is when you check your own credit report. When a landlord or employer checks your credit report, that too is considered a 'soft inquiry' which does not impact your credit score.

Another big misconception is that closing old and unused, but still active accounts will improve someone's credit score. This too is false. Having a long and positive credit history with a creditor actually boosts your score. Closing an account that you don't use but that contains positive information will actually hurt your score. You're better off not using the older account, but leaving it active.

Yet another misconception is that if someone has an old collection account on their credit report, if they pay it off, that the negative information will be automatically removed and boost your score. This too is untrue. Paying off old dept that went to collections will help you because the credit report will reflect a zero balance, but the fact that it was in collections will remain on your credit report (and continue to lower your score) for seven years, unless the creditor or collection agency chooses to remove that negative information once it's paid off or otherwise settled.

What is one of the worst mistakes you see people make when managing their credit?

Lucy: People ignore medical bills and that's a huge mistake. People often wind up in battles with their health insurance company and believe they're not responsible for the bills. Unpaid medical bills that go to collections, however, will appear on your credit report regardless of whether or not the insurance company was responsible for paying them. Thus, you're better off paying the medical bills and then negotiating with your insurance company. An unpaid medical bill, doctor's office bill or hospital bill that goes to collections will hurt your credit score. Do what's necessary to keep the unpaid medical bills from going to collections. You can often work out a payment plan with the creditor if you can't pay the entire bill at once.

Are there any other common mistakes you see people make?

Lucy: Yes. People run into problems with negative information being added to their credit report when they get divorced. The divorce decree does not automatically separate your credit card accounts or remove you from joint responsibility on other types of loans that you both obtained while married. As part of your divorce procedure, be sure to have your name removed from all joint accounts or have joint accounts closed. As long as a joint account remains open, if one person racks up charges on a joint credit card account, for example, both parties remain responsible, whether or not they're still married. I recommend closing joint accounts and opening up new accounts in just your name.

If you had an American Express card for ten years, for example, before going into the marriage and you added your spouses name to the account when you got married, now that you're divorced, you should have your spouse's name removed from the account. This will allow you to keep the account with a long and positive history open.

On a credit report, every consumer has the ability to add a short personal statement. Does this statement actually benefit the consumer in any way?

Lucy: A personal statement does not impact your credit score. It can, however, be beneficial to use a statement to explain a negative situation on your credit report if you know a credit grantor will be evaluating your actual credit report, not just your credit score.

Why have credit scores become so important in today's society?

Lucy: Someone's credit score is important because lenders have begun to reply on the scores heavily. If you want to benefit from the best credit deals, you typically need a credit score over 650. Different types of lenders evaluate someone's credit score differently. However, virtually all lending decisions are made these days based mainly on someone's credit score. This allows creditors to make fast, yet accurate decisions and often automate their decision making process to a large degree.

If someone is denied credit when they apply for a mortgage, a new credit card or a car loan, for example, what should they do next? What recourse do they have?

Lucy: If you're denied credit, you're automatically granted the ability to request a free copy of your credit report from the credit reporting agency whose information was used to deny you credit. Take advantage of the opportunity and request a copy of your credit report. Looking at your credit report, figure out what caused the red flags and figure out what you can do to fix the situation. Then, wait at least six months before you reapply for the credit if you've corrected the problem during that period. During the six months, pay all of your bills on-time and take other steps to improve your credit score. If you take steps to improve your credit, you will see improvement within a six month period if you handle things correctly.

Is there a point when someone's credit report or credit score can be so bad they should simply give up?

Lucy: There's no way to wipe your entire credit report clean and simply start over. A bankruptcy might eliminate some or all of your debt, but that information will remain on your credit report for up to ten years. You're better off taking on the attitude that you need to do what's necessary to slowly improve your credit over time. This could be a five-, seven- or ten-year process, but you need to start immediately and be persistent. Learn from your past credit mistakes and don't repeat them. Then, do what's necessary to pay off old debt and slowly repair your credit. Eventually, you will be able to wipe the slate clean. Everyone's situation is different, but if you begin taking an active roll in repairing your credit, you could see a jump in your credit score of up to 100 points or more in as little as 6 to 12 months.

Is there a difference among the three main credit reporting agencies in regard to how credit report data is collected and how each credit score is calculated?

Lucy: The process for collecting data about each consumer is basically the same. How the credit score is calculated, however, is different between the three bureaus. This is why when you review your credit scores from the three bureaus, they'll often be slightly different. New procedures are being implemented to calculate one single credit score, but for now, every consumer has three separate credit scores. Mortgage companies, for example, will often take the middle score from all three credit reporting agencies or the lower of two credit reporting agency scores when making their decisions. All three credit reporting agencies calculate credit scores based on a 300 to 850 scale, with 650 or above considered good credit. How the score is actually calculated differs, since each credit reporting agency uses a different formula. The actual formulas are

---

TIP

You can learn specifically how the score is calculated by each credit reporting agency by visiting MyFICO.com (www.myfico.com) web site.

---

considered proprietary. From the TrueCredit.com web site, you can learn about many of the factors that go into TransUnion's credit score calculation and the importance of each, based on how specific pieces of information are weighted within the calculation.

If someone needs help with credit repair or credit counseling, how can they best find a reputable company to work with and avoid scams?

Lucy: There is nothing a credit repair or credit counseling company can do for you that you can't do for yourself. That's important to remember. When you hire one of these companies, you have to pay them. You could pay someone to do the busy work, or you can invest the time to make the necessary calls and write the appropriate letters yourself. Consumers will often see ads for *debt consolidation, credit repair* services and *credit counseling*. Before choosing whom you'll work with, learn as much about the company and the services offered as possible. Many solutions offered by these companies involve consolidating your debt into one new loan, which the debt consolidation company then makes money on. Thus, it's important to shop around for the best deals and best services. Understand exactly what's being offered to you, what the costs are and how you'll benefit. Keep in mind that if you're involved with credit counseling and a company is representing you when negotiating with your creditors, your credit report

> **TIP**
>
>
>
> Chapter 10 offers more information about reliable organizations that provide credit counseling and debt consolidation.

will reflect this and it can negatively impact your credit score. Some creditors will not lend to consumers who have credit counseling services mentioned on their credit report.

What is "rapid rescoring" and how can it help a consumer's credit score?

Lucy: If you're applying for a mortgage, for example, and you take steps to improve your credit score, it will often take at least 30 days for updates or corrections to be made to your credit report and credit score. Mortgage brokers, for example, can hire independent agencies that offer 'rapid rescoring.' For a fee, a credit report and credit score can be updated in as little as 72 hours. This is legal and it does work, however, it can be a costly service. For some people who need to lock in a lower mortgage rate quickly, but need the updated and improved score to qualify after corrections have been made or outstanding debts have been paid or settled, this type of service can be beneficial and ultimately save a lot of money.

TIP

See Chapter 4 for details about the fee-based and free services offered by the three major credit reporting agencies for consumers.

What services does TrueCredit.com offer to consumers?

Lucy: TrueCredit is the consumer-oriented division of TransUnion. We offer credit reports, credit scores and credit report monitoring services through our web site (www.truecredit.com). We offer a variety of services, including a three-in-one credit report complete with credit score. We also offer a popular service which offers unlimited access to all three credit reports and credit scores, plus quick notification via email of changes made to your credit reports or score, for a flat monthly fee. This Unlimited 3-Bureau Reports with Credit Score service has a $24.95 start up fee, plus costs $14.95 per month. It includes $25,000 worth of identity theft insurance. Our paid services and free educational tools, newsletters and podcasts are available online only. From TransUnion, people can request a free copy of their credit report by telephone or in writing, however.

Maxine Sweet
Vice President of Public Education
Experian

Experian is one of the three major U.S. credit reporting agencies. For consumers, the company offers the Experian.com web site, which offers a variety of fee-based services and free educational tools. From this interview, you'll learn more about how credit reports and credit scores work and discover tips for better managing your own credit.

In terms of your personal credit score, the company also offers information at National Score Index (www.national scoreindex.com) web site, which explains credit scores and allows you to compare your score with others from around the country. From this web site you can quickly learn that the national average credit score is 678; however, in New England, for example, the average Experian credit score is 702 (as of March 2006). This web site also offers a variety of free online tools, including a debt payoff calculator, mortgage qualifier calculator, and tools to help you decide whether to lease or buy a car.

What's the difference between a credit reporting agency and a credit reporting company?

Maxine: Within the industry, we don't use the term 'credit reporting agency' any longer. It used to be that a credit reporting agency was a complete office located in a local community. Now, everything has been nationalized. We now refer to ourselves as a 'credit reporting company.' To determine who has access to your credit report and information compiled by the three credit reporting companies, I recommend someone refers to the list published within The Fair Credit Reporting Act (www.ftc.gov/os/statutes/fcra.htm).

How long does negative information stay on someone's credit report?

Maxine: Depending on the type of information, it will remain on a credit report for 7, 10, or 15 years. A credit report is designed to reflect not just where you are today from a credit and financial standpoint, but where you've been over time.

What can someone do when negative information appears on their credit report?

Maxine: The best thing you can do is contact the creditor and pay the debt. Even once a debt gets paid after it goes to collections, it will still reflect negatively on your credit report and credit score, but it will be weighed less heavily if it's paid. If the negative information is an error, that can be corrected within 30 days if you contact the creditor or the three credit reporting agencies directly. Typically, the fastest way to get a correction made is to dispute the error online.

What are the biggest misconceptions people have about their credit report and credit score?

Maxine: Many people believe that your credit score is a part of the credit report. This is false. A credit score is an additional tool that's made available by the credit reporting agencies. While your credit report and credit score can be obtained simultaneously, these are considered separate pieces of information. It's also necessary for people to understand that our scoring model for calculating someone's credit score is extremely complex and weighs different types of information differently. When calculating a credit score, a variety of factors are taken into account.

Another misconception is that student loans don't appear on your credit report, so it's okay to default on them. This is false. Student loans are just like car loans, mortgages, and other types of loans and should be treated accordingly. Also, when someone co-signs for a credit card or loan, that information appears on your credit report as well as the credit report of the person you co-signed for. Co-signing for a loan or credit card, for example, gives you equal responsibility for the debt. That information, positive or negative, will appear on your credit report and impact your credit score.

What can someone do to better understand how the credit score calculation is made and improve their credit score?

Maxine: The best a consumer can typically do is take advantage of the general advice and guidelines which are outlined on our web site (www.experian.com). Some of the things that most impact a credit score negatively include missed or late payments, how late the payments were made, how many payments were missed or late, and how long ago the payments were missed.

If someone has a lot of negative information on their credit report, what should they do to start improving their situation?

Maxine: I recommend first obtaining a copy of your credit report and credit score, so you know exactly where you stand. When you obtain your credit report from Experian as a consumer, we supply you with information pertaining to the positive and negative information on your report, so you can better understand your situation and how that data is influencing your credit score. As a consumer, one of the things you can control is your revolving credit, including your credit cards. You can determine how many credit card accounts you possess, the balances you maintain on each card, and whether you make timely payments. Maxing out your credit cards will lower your credit score. Having accounts with positive information open for a long period is beneficial. In the past, consumers were told to close old, unused credit accounts. This is no longer valid advice. It's now beneficial to maintain accounts in good standing, even if they're unused, over long periods of time.

What's a common mistake consumers make when managing their credit?

Maxine: People don't understand that every time a creditor checks their credit report, it impacts their credit score. So, if you apply for several different credit cards in a short period of time, that will actually hurt your credit score. There are instances when a credit inquiry by a creditor will not impact your score. For example, if you receive a 'pre-approved' credit card offer in the mail, because you didn't apply to be 'pre-approved,' your credit score is not penalized. Also if you're going car shopping, you can have an unlimited number of inquiries from car dealerships and car loan finance companies within a 30-day period. Those combined will count as one inquiry. The same is true with mortgages. The weight of inquiries on your credit score diminishes after several months.

How old should someone be when they begin to establish credit?

Maxine: As an adult, what's almost as bad as having bad information on your credit report is having no credit history at all. For this reason, I recommend to parents of high school and college students that they teach their children about managing credit early and help them establish their own credit between the ages of 18 and early-20s. A lot of credit card companies target college age students and offer them opportunities to establish their own credit. If a college student doesn't understand the responsibilities involved with having a credit card, however, they can easily mess up their credit report and credit score early in their lives. This is why credit and money management education is important. A responsible parent will teach their college-age children about credit, how it works and how to manage it properly. Don't reply on this important information being taught in school.

If someone is denied credit, what steps should they take?

Maxine: The first step is to determine which credit reporting agency the creditor used to make the decision. The rejection letter the consumer receives will include this, along with the primary reason or reasons why the application for credit or a loan was rejected. Next, contact that credit reporting agency and request a free copy of your credit report to ensure there are no errors on it. If the negative information is accurate, determine what you can do to begin fixing or improving the situation. If you notice an error on your credit report, it's in your best interest to have it corrected as quickly as possible by working with the creditor directly and then contacting the credit reporting agencies if your efforts at contacting or working with the creditor are unsuccessful.

Why has the credit score itself become so important?

Maxine: A credit report does not rate your credit. It only reports the facts about your credit and credit history. In the past, when you applied for credit, a human credit manager would have to carefully evaluate your detailed credit report manually and determine whether or not you were a qualified applicant for a loan or credit card, for example. When credit scores were created in the 1950s and widely implemented over the past few decades, this allowed creditors to redefine, often automate and dramatically speed up the credit approval process. The credit score system also allows consumers to be evaluated more objectively and fairly. Human biases are no longer part of the credit approval process, because often the automated process only evaluates someone's credit score.

What are some of the products and services Experian offers to consumers?

Maxine: There are three different ways someone can obtain a copy of their credit report from Experian. First, a consumer can contact our consumer assistance center. This is where someone is referred if they're declined for a loan or credit as a result of information we reported to a creditor. This is also the division consumers should contact if they believe they're victims of identity theft. Beyond requesting a free copy of their credit reports after being denied credit, consumers can purchase additional copies of their Experian credit report for $9.50. From the web site AnnualCreditReport.com, consumers are entitled to receive one free copy of their credit report per year from each of the credit reporting agencies. An alternative is to call (877) 322–8228 to request a free credit report. The second way someone can obtain a copy of their credit report is to consider the AnnualCreditReport.com web site or the toll-free number.

The third way to obtain your credit report is to pay a service for a three-in-one credit report or subscribe to a credit monitoring service which notifies you every time a change is made to your credit report. These services are typically offered on a monthly subscription basis and provide unlimited access to your credit report and/or credit score from either one or all three of the credit reporting agencies, depending on the service you subscribe to. The Experian web site (www.experian.com) offers a variety of fee-based services to consumers, as well as free online educational tools.

If consumers need help with credit repair or credit counseling, how can they best find a reputable company to work with and avoid the scams?

Maxine: Consumers beware is the advice I have to offer when it comes to companies offering 'credit repair' services. Beware of any company that claims it can fix your credit. There are a lot of scams surrounding credit repair services. Some companies promote fraudulent activities to have negative but accurate information removed from a credit report. It's important for a consumer to understand that any legitimate service that offers credit counseling or credit repair should only offer legal services that anyone can also do for themselves. There are a lot of companies that operate outside of the law when it comes to offering illegitimate services to people with credit problems.

What is the difference between debt consolidation and credit counseling services?

Maxine: Debt consolidation is a profit-oriented service where the consumer takes out one interest bearing loan to pay off other outstanding loans or debt. If you pursue this route, make sure you understand the fees and interest rates of the new loan and that you work with a reputable company. A debt management or credit counseling service helps people who are in serious financial trouble negotiate with their creditors to settle debts, obtain lower interest rates, and reduce fees. These services work on your behalf, for a fee. Working with a debt management or credit counseling company reflects negatively on your credit report and it's important to find a reputable company to work with. The benefit to using one of these services is that you'll be educated about how to fix your credit problems and receive the assistance you need to do this. When looking for a reputable service, consider obtaining a referral from The National Foundation for Credit Counseling (www.nfcc.org).

Do you have any last-minute advice to consumers relating to credit reports?

Maxine: Your credit report is a financial tool you can use to your advantage. It's not something you should be afraid of. By understanding the importance of your credit report and the information it provides, you can better manage your credit and teach yourself to become a more credit-worthy consumer.

Credit-Related
Resources

The following is a summary of important contacts and web sites described within this book:

Annual Credit Report Request Service
P.O. Box 105281
Atlanta, GA 30348-5281
(877) 322-8228
www.annualcreditreport.com

Better Business Bureau
www.bbb.org

Certified Financial Planner Board of Standards
www.cfp.com

Credit Card Comparison Sites
www.cardratings.com
www.creditcards.com
www.creditcardscenter.com
www.e-wisdom.com/credit_cards/chart.html, www.lower
mybills.com

Credit Card Optimization Calculator
www.myfico.com/CreditEducation/Calculators/Card
Optimizer.aspx

Debt Consolidation Loan Calculator
www.lowermybills.com/servlet/LMBServlet?the_action=
NavigateDebtConsolidationLoansAppFirstStep

Equifax
(800) 685-1111
www.equifax.com

Experian
(888) 397-3742
www.experian.com

Fair Isaac Corporation (FICO Score)
www.MyFICO.com

Federal Fair Debt Collection Practices Act
www.ftc.gov/os/statutes/fdcpa/fdcpact.htm

Federal Trade Commission (credit information)
(877) 382-4357
www.ftc.gov/credit

FICO Score Estimator
www.bankrate.com/brm/fico/calc.asp

Identity Theft Data Clearing House
(877) ID-THEFT
www.consumer.gov/idtheft

Loan Savings Calculator
www.myfico.com/myfico/CreditCentral/LoanRates.asp#
Calculator

The National Foundation for Consumer Credit
(800) 388-2227
www.nfcc.org

TransUnion
(800) 916-8800
www.transunion.com

Glossary of
Credit-Related Terms

Annual Credit Report Request Service. A centralized service operated by the three credit reporting agencies (credit bureaus) that processes all requests from consumers who wish to receive their free credit reports from each agency. This can be done online, by phone, or by mail.

Annual Fee. Related to credit cards, this is a fee that's charged to the consumer every year for the privilege of having a specific credit card. Depending on the card, the annual fee might range from free to $150 per year. Ideally, you want a credit card with no annual fee. If the card has some type of reward for usage (such as airline miles) or a cash back bonus tied to it, an annual fee will often apply.

Annual Percentage Rate (APR). This is a measure of the cost of credit, expressed as a yearly interest rate. This is the amount of interest you'll pay per year on your balance from purchases for that card. The APR could be different if you use the card for cash advances or transfer a balance from another card.

Average Daily Balance. This is the method the credit card issuer uses to calculate your payment due. Your average daily balance is determined by adding each day's balance and then dividing that total by the number of days in a billing cycle. Your average daily balance is then multiplied by a card's monthly periodic rate, which is calculated by dividing the APR by 12.

Balance Transfer and Balance Transfer Rate. A balance transfer involves moving an outstanding balance from one credit card, presumably to a lower interest credit card to save money. (The balance would remain the same, but you'd then be paying a lower interest rate.) In order to entice consumers to utilize this, many credit card issues offer a special incentive or teaser rate on balance transfers. Keep in mind, however, there can also be additional fees associated with balance transfers, so understand the terms and conditions on both credit cards. The Balance Transfer Rate is the APR you'll receive on the amount of money you transfer to the new card. If you're being offered a special teaser rate, determine what the APR will be when that teaser rate expires. Read the Card Holder Agreement carefully.

Card Holder Agreement. This is the "fine print" associated with each credit card. It lists all of the terms and conditions, fees and other information a card holder should know pertaining to the use of that card. All fees, for example, will be listed within the Card Holder Agreement.

Cash Advance Fee. Many credit cards are accompanied by an ATM PIN (Personal Identification Number) which allows you to obtain cash advances using that credit card. Depending on the credit card issuer, there might be a flat fee associated with each ATM transaction, or you could be charged a percentage of the amount withdrawn (and possibly a flat fee as well). Withdrawing money from an ATM using a credit card is referred to as a "cash advance." Often, the portion of your outstanding credit card balance that's a result of cash advances will be charged a higher APR. Read the Card Holder Agreement associated with the credit card carefully.

Credit. When someone borrows money with the understanding it will be repaid, that person is given credit. Obtaining credit from a creditor has costs associated with it. The cost is incurred based on the interest rate and fees you'll be required to pay over time, in addition to the principal. Although the interest rate can be pre-set or variable, how much you ultimately pay will also be determined by the amount of time it takes you to fully repay the loan, whether it's a mortgage, credit card, car loan, or any other type of loan. There are many forms of loans and credit and each works slightly differently.

Credit Card Transaction Fees. These are extra fees you'll need to pay to use your credit card for certain types of transactions, such as ATM (cash advance) withdrawals, making a late payment, or going over your credit limit.

Credit Counseling. A service that teaches you how to better manage your finances and that can negotiate with your creditors on your behalf to help you regain your financial stability and rebuild your credit. There are often fees associated with credit counseling services, even if the organization you work with is a nonprofit corporation.

Credit Rating. From a potential lender's standpoint, someone's credit rating is an estimate or educated guess relating to credit worthiness—whether you'll repay your debt on time, with the appropriate interest. Your credit rating is a prediction regarding the likelihood of interest and capital actually being paid back and of the extent to which the lender is protected in the event of default. This numerical score (between 300 and 850) is calculated based on your credit (financial) reputation and history with creditors in the past.

Credit Report. Compiled by one of the credit reporting agencies, such as Equifax, Experian, or TransUnion, a credit report contains personal and financial information about you, including your name, address, phone number, social security number, date of birth, past addresses, current and past employers, a listing of companies that have issued you credit (including credit cards, charge cards, car loans, mortgages, student loans, home equity loans, etc.), and details about your credit history (whether or not you pay your bills on time.) Each of the major credit reporting agencies compiles a separate credit report for every individual. However, much of the information on each report should be identical or similar.

Credit Reporting Agency (aka Credit Bureau). The three national bureaus that maintain credit reports on virtually all Americans with any type of credit history are Equifax, Experian, and TransUnion. These agencies maintain vast databases that are updated regularly. Their purpose is to supply creditors with timely and reliable financial information about individual consumers. It's important to understand that a credit reporting agency does *not* decide whether an individual qualifies for credit or not. Credit reporting agencies simply collect information that is relevant to a person's credit history and habits and then provides that information (for a fee), in the form of a credit report, to creditors and lenders.

Credit Score. Using a complex formula that's calculated based on many criteria related to your current financial situation and credit history, the three major credit reporting agencies calculate and regularly update your credit score. According to the Federal Trade Commission, "Most creditors use credit scoring to evaluate your credit record. This involves using your credit application and report to get information about you, such as your annual income, outstanding debt, bill paying history, and the number and types of accounts you have and how long you have had them. Potential lenders use your credit score to help predict whether you are a good risk to repay a loan and make payments on time." TransUnion reports someone's credit score is, "a mathematical calculation that reflects a consumer's creditworthiness. The score is an assessment of how likely a consumer is to pay his or her debts."

Debt Consolidation. This involves taking out a new, larger loan at one predetermined interest rate, so that you can pay off outstanding debts that are overdue and/or that potentially are charging much higher interest rates.

Debt Management Plan (DMP). A credit counseling service can help you create and implement a formal and personalized debt management plan, or DMP, which can be used to systematically pay off your debt over an extended period of time.

Debt Negotiation Service. Like a credit counseling company, a debt negotiation service will help you make contact with your specific creditors and negotiate on your behalf to help you pay off or settle your debt, depending on the circumstances.

Dispute. If you find an error in the information listed on your credit report, you have a right to initiate a *dispute* with the creditor and/or credit reporting agency. By law, a dispute must be investigated within 30 days. If the information is, in fact, inaccurate, it must then be corrected, causing your credit report and potentially your credit score to be revised.

Fair Debt Collection Act. Legislation passed by the federal government that outlines the legal rights of consumers, lenders, creditors, and collection agencies.

Federal Trade Commission (FTC). This branch of the U.S. government deals with issues that relate directly to the economic lives of most Americans. The Bureau of Consumer Protection, which operates under the FTC, is responsible for protecting consumers against unfair, deceptive, or fraudulent practices. The Bureau enforces a variety of consumer protection laws enacted by Congress, as well as trade regulation rules issued by the Commission. The FTC is in charge of enforcing the Fair Debt Collection Act, which prohibits debt collectors from engaging in unfair, deceptive, or abusive practices, including over-charging, harassment, and disclosing consumers' debt to third parties.

Grace Period. For someone who has a zero balance on his or her credit card, who then uses the card to make purchases during a given month, the grace period is the time between the day the purchases are made and when finances charges (interest, etc.) will start being added to the new balance. A grace period is typically between 20 and 30 days. If no grace period is offered, finance charges will accrue starting the moment a purchase is made with the credit card. For someone who already has a balance on his or her credit card, a grace period does not apply.

Identity Theft. This is the unauthorized use of personal identification information to commit fraud or other crimes. This could include someone using your credit card(s) to make unauthorized purchases or using your identity to take out loans or establish credit in your name.

Minimum Payment. This is the lowest amount a credit card holder must pay to keep his or her credit card account from going into default (and being reported negatively to the credit reporting agencies). The minimum payment is typically about 2 percent (or 2.5 percent) of the outstanding balance.

Mortgage. A mortgage is a long-term loan that's secured by the collateral of a specific real estate property. The borrower is obliged to make a predetermined series of payments to cover the principal, interest, and any related fees.

National Foundation for Credit Counseling (NFCC). This organization is the country's largest and longest serving national nonprofit credit counseling organization. The NFCC's mission is to set the national standard for quality credit counseling, debt reduction services, and education for financial wellness through its member agencies.

Over-the-Limit Fee. Related to credit cards, if your charges and fees combined go over your credit limit in any given billing cycle, you will be assessed this additional fee. Many credit card issuers charge a $35 over-the-limit fee.

Trade Line. Each item listed on your credit report is called a Trade Line, whether it's a mortgage, car loan, student loan, credit card, charge card, or other type of loan. For each Trade Line, you will see detailed information on your credit report.

Index

ANF 332.7 RICH

Rich, J.
Dirty little secrets.

PRICE: $15.95 (9024/ANF